THE BIBLE
in Art

THE OLD TESTAMENT

THE BIBLE
in Art

THE OLD TESTAMENT

RICHARD MÜHLBERGER

PORTLAND HOUSE
New York

Copyright © 1991 Moore & Moore Publishing

This 1991 edition was published by Portland House, a division of Dilithium Press, Ltd., distributed by Outlet Book Company, Inc, a Random House Company, 225 Park Avenue South, New York, New York 10003

8 7 6 5 4 3 2 1

ISBN 0-517-03746-7

Printed and bound in Hong Kong

The Bible in Art: The Old Testament was prepared and produced by Moore & Moore Publishing, 11 W. 19th Street, New York, New York 10011

Photo Credits

Art Gallery of New South Wales, Sydney 140-141; The Art Institute of Chicago 16-17; Artothek 26, 89, 132-133; Ashmolean Museum 116; Bildarchiv Preussischer Kulturbesitz 138; BKL Photographie (Photograph by Jean Bernard) 56; Bridgeman Art Library/SuperStock, Inc. 10-11, 43, 82, 150; The Chrysler Museum 42; Cincinnati Art Museum 130; City of Bristol Museum and Art Gallery 103; City of Manchester Art Galleries 102; Collection of Piero Corsini 58, 59; Dulwich Picture Gallery 68-69, 122-123; Evansville Museum of Arts and Science 126; Richard L. Feigen & Co. (Photographs by Gregory W. Schmitz) 70-71, 106, 108, 146-147; The Fine Arts Museums of San Francisco 165; Fotowerstatt, Hamburger Kunsthalle (Photograph by Elke Walford) 12; The J. Paul Getty Museum 74-75; Indianapolis Museum of Art 63, 86-87; Bob Jones University 83; Kunsthistorishes Museum, Vienna 124-125; Landesmuseum Mainz 113; Los Angeles County Museum of Art 114, 156; The Metropolitan Museum of Art 22-23, 24, 49; Museo de Arte de Ponce, Puerto Rico 109; Museo del Prado 18, 19; Museum of Fine Arts, Boston 119, 143; Museum of Fine Arts, Springfield 84, 110-111; The National Gallery London 50, 54, 55, 72, 99, 121, 154-155, 162, 168-169; National Gallery of Art, Washington, D.C. 28, 36-37, 52-53, 80, 90, 94, 120, 128-129, 141, 145, 157; National Gallery of Canada 115; National Gallery of Scotland 60-61; National Museum of American Art, Smithsonian Institution 158-159; The Newark Museum 25; Oronoz, SA 64-65; Réunion des Musées Nationaux/Copyright Artist's Rights Society 96; Réunion des Musées Nationaux 136-137; Rijksmuseum Van Gogh, Amsterdam 46-47; Rijksmuseum, Amsterdam 57, 98; John & Mable Ringling Museum of Art 44-45; Salander-O'Reilly Galleries, Inc. 149; San Antonio Museum Association 33; Staatliche Kunsthalle Karlsruhe 95; Staatliche Kunstsammlungen Kassel 66-67, 76-77; Staatsgalerie Stuttgart 127; Städelsches Kunstitut, Frankfurt 112; Stadtische Galerie im Lenbachhaüs 30-31; Statens Museum for Kunst, Copenhagen 166-167; SuperStock, Inc. 14-15, 20-21, 32, 38-39, 40-41, 91, 97, 144, 148, 152, 153, 163; Worcester Art Museum 88, 170

PAGE 2 CHAGALL: *Moses Receiving the Tablets of the Law* (detail)

AN M&M BOOK

Project Director & Editor: Gary Fishgall

Senior Editorial Assistant: Shirley Vierheller; *Editorial Assistants:* Maxine Dormer, Ben D'Amprisi, Jr; *Copyediting:* Bert N. Zelman, Keith Walsh of Publishers Workshop Inc; *Photo Research:* Maxine Dormer, Jana Marcus, Janice Ostan.

Designer: Binns & Lubin

Separations and Printing: Regent Publishing Services Ltd.

Measurements of the paintings are in inches, height before width.

Contents

Introduction   6

Beginnings 8

Patriarchs   34

Out of Egypt   78

Heroes and Heroines   104

Wise Men and Prophets   134

The Apocrypha   160

About the Artists 171

Index to Artists and Illustrations   176

The books of the Old Testament form one of the oldest literary works in recorded history. And one of the most celebrated. No painting or poem or symphony is better known than some of the passages penned by the patriarchs, prophets, and psalmists who wrote the Hebrew Bible. The images formed by their words are powerful. But the lives, loves, battles, and miracles of the Bible happened so long ago that for many people they do not seem real until an artist gives them life. Those rare and talented individuals who can render in paint the attitudes, mores, and events of a distant past help to keep the Bible as vital as the faith it inspires. And their works of art speak not only to the audiences for whom they were originally intended, but also to those who view them today—the faithful and those with no religious inclinations at all. It is the intent of this book to celebrate such creativity.

For many centuries works of art inspired by the Old Testament were rare since Jewish law forbade the worship of graven images. Instead, the Hebrews found compensation in a rich tradition of storytelling and in the singing of sacred texts. The Hebrew Bible was its own art form. However, the advent of Christianity brought forth a desire to match words with images, and since then the texts of the Old Testament have held a place in art equal to those of the Gospels and Epistles. Equal but different. Until the 20th century, paintings of Christian subjects were traditionally tied to the yearly cycle of readings that celebrated Jesus' life, death, and resurrection. Meanwhile Old Testament subjects found impetus in two primary sources of patronage—the Church, which commissioned or inspired works because of their connection to the story of redemption, and the royal princes, who were interested in themes that conveyed moral lessons or models for just rule. In our own age, artists have been drawn to metaphors that link the struggles and triumphs of the Hebrew nation with the concerns and joys of contemporary living.

The stories of the Old Testament came into their own in Florence in the 15th century when David was adopted as a symbol of that small, proud Italian city. Prior to the Renaissance, subjects from the Hebrew Bible were generally subservient to the Christian stories or were used to prefigure the New Testament scenes with which they were paired. The rare exceptions do not form a cohesive body of work and, hence, appear awkward when viewed with later treatments passed down, as it were, from one generation of artists to the next. Therefore, the paintings chosen for this book date from the Renaissance and later. They demonstrate changes in style from era to era, as well as differing approaches to the sacred texts. In choosing from the countless works of art that cover the subject, a decided preference was made in favor of paintings with a strong psychological content. This author believes that when an artist gets into the "skin" of his characters, the Bible truly comes to life. Not all artists are equally adept at playacting in this fashion, but the weaker thespians compensate for their shortcomings through technical virtuosity or a seductive use of color and texture. No matter what the means, it is storytelling based on an authentic understanding of the people in the sacred texts that enriches these pages. It is all meant to delight the eye and enrich the soul.

In giving initial consideration to the scope of this volume, it was decided to include works inspired by The Apocrypha, the collection of 14 short inspirational and historical works written by Greek-speaking Jews in the years between 200 B.C. and A.D. 100. Because they were written long after the rest of the Hebrew Bible, these stories were rejected by the Jews at the Council of Jamnia in A.D. 90 when the biblical canon was finally settled. While accepting Jewish opinion that the stories were "apocryphal," and not the true word of God, Christians valued them as a link between the Old and New Testaments. Martin Luther, for example, defended them as good reading for the pious, although his followers eventually rejected them because they believed with the Jews that they were largely fictitious. Artists, of course, stayed out of the fray. They heard the apocryphal stories in church and were drawn to the bravery of its heroes, particularly Judith, Susanna, and Tobit. Consequently art is rich in scenes from the apocryphal stories. To overlook such works in this volume, it was felt, would be to ignore a rich and significant body of art. Nevertheless, the stories of the Apocrypha and the selected paintings inspired by them have been kept separate from the rest of this volume and readers should understand that these stories are not to be found in the Hebrew Bible or in the Protestant Old Testament.

For 25 years, the author has had the pleasure of introducing a wide range of people to the treasures of art. The present volume and its companion, *The Bible in Art: The New Testament*, reflect the sum of that experience, whose principal tenet is that every work of art has something to say. Words, however, are often necessary to translate that meaning to an audience. The right words come from study of an artist's life, times, and intentions, but, more importantly, they come from looking. Close, empathetic looking. Almost every work of art in this volume is housed in an art museum or gallery, and the reader is encouraged to visit these paintings if the opportunity to do so arises. No matter how faithfully one reproduces images in a book, there is simply no substitute for seeing an actual work of art. Somehow a painting on the wall of a museum has a pulse and a vitality that no reproduction on the page of a book can equal. The original will always be a surprise, and the hand of the artist can always be better appreciated in the temples that are dedicated to his craft. Nevertheless, in this volume, the large sizes of many of the illustrations, and the inclusion of numerous details, represent an effort to simulate as much as possible the act of viewing a painting in the flesh.

It is also sincerely hoped that the brief synopses of the Biblical stories in this book, accompanied by frequent quotations from the Scriptures, will encourage readers to go back to the original source material and to enjoy again—or perhaps for the first time—the literary power and beauty they contain. The source used herein is the Revised Standard Version, simply because it is the most popular of all the modern translations. Other versions, however, are also recommended, particularly the King James Version of 1611 if poetry is desired. While most of the stories in this volume are arranged in chronological order, some slight license has been taken here and there to bring groups of related subjects together.

Gary Fishgall, the editor at M & M Books, conceived the idea for this volume and its New Testament companion. He has guided the author and helped him immensely in his presentation of the art and in the accompanying text. Maxine Dormer, Mr. Fishgall's assistant, was unrelentingly reliable in tracking down transparencies from all over Europe and America, and in keeping production details in careful order. The author wishes to thank them both. He dedicates this volume to the friend who most inspired him to keep reading, looking, and writing, Miss Grace Fletcher.

Beginnings

The Creation

In keeping with the Third Commandment—"You shall not make for yourself a graven image, or any likeness of any thing that is in heaven above . . ." (Exodus 20:4)—artists refrained from depicting the image of God until the 11th century A.D. By the Renaissance, however, his presence in paintings as the "Ancient of Days" was common, as were depictions of him as emperor or pope. These paintings were not seen as idols—and therefore in contradiction to the Lord's commandment—but rather as aids to worship. Of these depictions, perhaps none were more immediately and overwhelmingly successful than the five great images of God the Creator painted by Michelangelo on the ceiling of the Sistine Chapel in Rome. Inspired by a figure of Jupiter from the early second century A.D., the Renaissance master depicted the Almighty with the face and beard of an old man, canonizing for all time this iconography.

In one of the Sistine images, *God Dividing the Waters and the Earth,* the Lord is cocooned in the folds of his own cloak, and supported by naked youths. Although the Holy Scripture suggests that God brought forth the sun and the moon, the earth and the sky, and man and the animals by calling out their names, Michelangelo's vision is one of stupendous silence. God, like the artist, creates with his hands. Here it is a hand of blessing, one that brings forth continents and oceans out of an earth that was "without form and void" (Genesis 1:2). Michelangelo, seemingly inspired by this notion, makes energetic, formless marks with his brush along the edge of the oval that surrounds the figures, as though even God's robe is in the process of being formed along with the continents and oceans.

God Dividing the Waters and the Earth
MICHELANGELO BUONARROTI, Italian, 1475–1564
Vatican Museums and Galleries, Rome. Fresco: detail, Ceiling of the Sistine Chapel

PRECEDING PAGES

NATOIRE:*The Expulsion from Paradise* (detail)

The Creation of Eve

HENRY FUSELI, Anglo-Swiss, 1741–1825

Hamburger Kunsthall, Hamburg, Germany. Oil on canvas, 119 ³/₄ x 80 ³/₄ in.

After giving life to man and the animals, God decided that his human creation should have a mate. So he placed Adam in a deep sleep, removed one of his ribs, and closed its place with flesh. From the rib, he made a woman, Eve.

The Creation of Eve by Henry Fuseli re-creates this dramatic moment. In a conception that is as original as it is theatrical, God is shown as a classical giant, detached from his work as he communicates with the unknown above. Meanwhile Eve, in contrast to the surgical description of the Genesis story, is seen floating upward as she leaves Adam's side. Her first act is the worship of her Creator.

Fuseli was a Swiss artist (born Johann Heinrich Füssli) who spent most of his adult life in England. As with many learned men of his age, he was interested in the "sublime," a new aesthetic concept that concerned itself with man's feelings when confronted with the awe and vastness of the natural world, heroic acts, or the work of God. What was considered sublime in 18th-century theory was distinct from the merely beautiful or the picturesque; it usually involved a high level of drama and mystery. In order to express this quality in art, Fuseli turned for inspiration to the work of Michelangelo, which he studied firsthand and in great depth during a sojourn in Italy from 1770 to 1778. Thus in *The Creation of Eve*, Fuseli attenuates his figures in the manner of the Italian Renaissance master and skillfully curves them into a composition of elegant, yearning forms. His adoring Eve shows the wonder that a human being would be likely to feel in the presence of the deity, while the murky figure of God and the darkness surrounding him are effective evocations of awe.

Fuseli achieved popular success during his own lifetime but was ignored by the Victorians who found his art too eccentric. It was not until the 20th century, when he was seen as a kindred spirit by the Surrealists and Expressionists, that his work again found a serious audience among art lovers. It is appreciated today for its startling originality and for its sincerity of expression.

The Garden of Eden

After God created man and a garden to serve as his home and work place, he established one unbreakable rule—that Adam not eat the fruit of "the tree of the knowledge of good and evil." "In the day that you eat of it," he warned, "you shall die" (Genesis 2:17). Then woman was created, and she too learned of God's rule.

Adam and Eve were content to follow the Lord's dictum until a serpent—the most subtle of all the wild creatures—tempted Eve to sample the fruit. "You will not die," the wily reptile said. "God knows that when you eat of it your eyes will be opened and you will be like God, knowing good and evil." So Eve ate. Then she gave the fruit to her husband, who ate as well. Suddenly the man and the woman became aware of their nakedness, and clothed themselves with fig leaves. Upon hearing the voice of God, however, they hid. But the Lord demanded to know what had happened, so they fearfully told him their story—Adam blaming Eve, and she blaming the serpent. Enraged by their betrayal, God cursed the serpent, forcing it to spend its life on its belly, eating dust; to the woman he gave the pain of childbirth; and to the man he promised a lifetime of toil. He then drove Adam and Eve out of the garden.

In *The Garden of Paradise* by Hieronymus Bosch, the story of Man's first sin is told in a serial way. In the right foreground, Adam sleeps while Eve rises to her feet under the gentle guidance of her maker. In the middle distance to the left, the serpent introduces Adam and Eve to the fruit of the tree. And on the right side of the painting, the hapless pair leave Paradise. These depictions conform to conventional versions of the story, even to the portrait of the serpent as half human. But the artist's idea of the Garden of Eden is unique. It seems to combine the workmanship of a jeweler with the mound-building skills of an army of ants. And Bosch's fountain is so fantastic that it resembles more a dream witnessed by the sleeping Adam than the real source of the four rivers of Paradise. Of course, one must remember that when Bosch created this work in the days before the Protestant Reformation, devilry and witchcraft were considered as real as trees and flowers. Therefore, his vision was probably not as startling nor as unique to his contemporaries as it is to the modern eye.

About a hundred years after Bosch combined fantasy with narrative to help his audience contemplate the wonder and power of God, two of his countrymen depended on gorgeous realism to achieve the same end. Peter Paul Rubens painted the human figures in *Adam and Eve in Paradise*, and Jan Bruegel the Elder was responsible for the animals and landscape. So splendid, ordered, and infinitely varied is their creation that one might overlook the forbidden fruit in Eve's hands.

(continued on page 16)

FOLLOWING PAGES
Adam and Eve in Paradise
PETER PAUL RUBENS, Flemish, 1577–1640, and JAN BRUEGEL THE ELDER, Flemish, 1568–1625'
Koninklijk Kabinet van Schilderijen "Mauritshuis", The Hague. Oil on wood panel, 28 7/8 x 44 1/2 in.

DETAIL
Adam and Eve in Paradise

While the contemporaries of Bosch accepted the master's images on face value alone, symbolic as well as literal meanings could be found in the work of Rubens and Bruegel. In *Adam and Eve in Paradise*, for example, most of the animals near the master and mistress of Eden represent qualities beyond themselves. The horse next to Adam signifies his nobility, while the dog at Eve's feet refers to her marital fidelity. Rabbits are symbols of fecundity, the eyes in the peacock's tail feathers represent the eyes of God, the little monkey symbolizes sin and the devil, and the two parrots in the tree are creatures who copy what others say, just as Adam copies Eve's action in tasting the fruit. The satanic serpent, however, is simply depicted as a snake coiled around a branch of the tree of knowledge.

Hieronymus Bosch is considered one of the most imaginative artists ever to live; Peter Paul Rubens is remembered as one of the most pleasing and influential; and Jan Bruegel the Elder is one of the greatest masters of still-life painting. Bosch drew his inspiration from medieval works of meditation and the tiny images that decorate these manuscripts. Rubens and Bruegel drew from nature and represent a more scientific approach to subject matter. The fame of all three, however, depended on their ability to transform history and nature into images more wonderful than anything seen before.

The Garden of Paradise

HIERONYMUS BOSCH, Dutch, ca. 1450–1516

Robert A. Waller Memorial Fund, The Art Institute of Chicago. Oil and tempera on wood panel, 10 5/8 x 15 15/16 in.

Adam and Eve

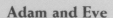

While Adam and Eve have been the subject of art for centuries, artists before the Renaissance focused on the couple's fall. In *Adam and Eve* by Albrecht Dürer, however, the first man and woman emerge as human beauty perfected.

It was a trip to Italy, the wellspring of the Renaissance, that gave Dürer the inspiration for this work. The German painter arrived in the South during the winter of 1505. At the time, he was relatively well known, thanks to his extraordinary output of woodcuts and engravings (one of which depicted Adam and Eve but as much chubbier than they appear here). After executing a commission for German merchants in Venice, he sought out artists who had worked with Leonardo da Vinci, and probably attempted to see the great artist himself but was unsuccessful in doing so. From those who knew the master, however, he learned Leonardo's system for depicting human proportions, a system that dated back to the ancient Greeks and made the size of the head the basis for measuring the rest of the body. Dürer utilized the canon of proportions in his *Adam and Eve*. The figure of Adam, for example, is seven heads tall. His sun-bronzed coloring—darker than that of Eve—is also derived from the art techniques of antiquity.

Dürer has indeed created two classically perfect beings, a prince and princess for Eden. But it is the way he poses the two figures that gives these paintings their individuality and their fame.

Adam is exceedingly tentative in his stance. He probes for secure grounding with his right foot while extending the fingers of his right hand as though to test the space around him before venturing into it. His head is slightly thrown back, and turned in a three-quarters profile. Locks of his golden hair stream behind him. The overall impression is that Adam has materialized on the spot, and one wonders whether he will stay or not. He is linked to Eve by the branch of fruit that dangles

Adam
ALBRECHT DÜRER, German, 1471–1528

Museo del Prado, Madrid. Oil on wood panel,
82 ¹/₈ x 31 ¹/₈ in.

from his fingers. He turns to her, as though for the very first time, to ask perhaps what the fruit is called. The apple at this moment seems more a symbol of fecundity than of sin.

Eve smiles to herself as a young girl might while concentrating on the mastery of a difficult ballet movement. Indeed, with her left foot directly behind the right, her stance resembles that of a dancer. She grasps a branch of the tree for balance and nonchalantly accepts an apple from the serpent without even glancing at it. Dürer's "calling card" conspicuously hangs from the same branch as that which hides Eve's nakedness. The earth beneath her—and Adam as well—seems like a moonscape, and the pitch-black background gives one the feeling that these lovely creatures have just been born of the cosmos. Of the two, Eve seems the more natural, apparently capable of following God's dictum to "be fruitful and multiply." Adam, on the other hand, looks as though he might view conception as more of an intellectual exercise than a physical act. If both figures continue their movements, taking just two more steps, they will face one another directly and be able to cleave to one another, becoming "one flesh," as God intended (Genesis 2:24).

Edvard Munch's painting of 1908, almost four hundred years later than Dürer's masterpiece, was one of a number of works in which the celebrated Scandinavian artist grappled with his feelings about fertility and life; it also presaged his struggle in the years 1933–1935—at the age of seventy—with the concept of jealousy. In *Adam and Eve Under the Apple Tree*, the subjects stand apart by more than an arm's length, seemingly wanting to move closer to one another, but timid and distrustful. Eve is languidly relaxed, absentmindedly

Eve

ALBRECHT DÜRER, German, 1471–1528

Museo del Prado, Madrid. Oil on wood panel, 82 1/8 x 31 1/8 in.

holding a branch of the apple tree for balance as she searches the face of the fruit as though it might contain a message. Adam thrusts his hands into his pockets, assuming an awkward stance that suggests stubbornness as well as anticipation. "You know you mustn't eat that," he seems to say, "but if you do, let me have a bite, too." Originally the figures were unclothed, but ultimately Munch draped them, opting for the freedom to express their relationship and feelings through body language rather than abide by the constraints that a puritan Norway would have placed on their naked depiction. The serpent is not shown, but the twist of the branches directly behind Adam's shoulder suggests a plump snake.

While Albrecht Dürer saw the first humans as the foremost embodiments of masculine and feminine beauty, Munch is more concerned with their psychological states. His young Lord and Lady of Eden, handsome though they are, are engaged in internal emotional struggles. Thus, while Dürer cannot conceive of his beautiful creatures sinning, even after they eat the forbidden fruit, Munch suggests that only in sin will they perhaps find fulfillment.

Adam and Eve under the Apple Tree
EDVARD MUNCH, Norwegian, 1863–1944
Oslo Kommunes Kunstfamlinger, Norway. Oil on canvas, 50 ³/₈ x 78 ⁷/₈ in.

The Expulsion From Paradise

Except for one verse stating that Adam and Eve "were both naked, and were not ashamed" (Genesis 2:25), the delights of life in the Garden of Eden were ignored by the Book of Genesis. Over the centuries, artists have preferred to dwell a little longer in Paradise, taking great pleasure in depicting the nudity of its inhabitants. In fact, many of them so enjoyed the opportunity to portray human perfection that even after the Fall they failed to add the aprons of fig leaves that Adam and Eve created to hide their shame.

Such is the case in *The Creation of the World and the Expulsion of Adam and Eve from Paradise*, in which Giovanni di Paolo follows the artistic convention of showing the first humans nude. But everything else in his remarkable depiction of earthly perfection is unique. He was particularly adventurous in using this work to contrast the cosmic with the human and to view the Earth from close up and from afar. That he did so in one small panel painting is even more remarkable.

In the left portion of the picture, under God the Father, one can see a great orb representing Eden's order and seclusion. At its center is a startling "map" of the Earth, which Giovanni conceived as circular, if not spherical (Giovanni's activity as a painter ended a decade before the first voyage of Christopher Columbus). The rings around the orb resemble a charting of atmospheric layers, but such a concept was unknown in Giovanni's day. Rather they most likely represent the cosmology of *The Divine Comedy*, Dante's masterpiece, which was widely read by the Italian intelligentsia at the time.

God seems to be spinning the circle of creation toward the confused couple, who are hurrying out of its path at the behest of a nervous and eager angel. But for his halo and wings, this heavenly creature could be

The Creation of the World and the Expulsion from Paradise

GIOVANNI DI PAOLO, Italian, active 1420–1482

The Metropolitan Museum of Art, The Robert Lehman Collection, 1975, New York. Tempera and gold on wood panel, 18 ¹⁵/₁₆ x 20 ¹/₂ in.

the big brother of Adam and Eve, so similar is he to them in coloring and facial appearance. The earth under their feet is a tapestry of flowers and rabbits from which seven stately trees of golden fruit emerge to form a screen against the purest of azure skies. God's radiance casts a golden glow over this blue backdrop.

The composition is almost self-consciously symmetrical in its diagonal divisions: God and Man fill two quadrants; the symbols of Paradise fill the remainder. Wavy patterns summarily painted by Giovanni to represent the four rivers that flow from Eden occupy the lower right corner of the painting and are balanced in the upper left by the wings of the incorporeal blue creatures who propel God into the scene. But it is God's firm and controlled anger, as he commands the angel to rid Paradise of the sinning humans, and the surprised reaction of Adam and Eve to the angel's shoving, that transform the painting from a decorative and intellectual exercise into one of human dimensions. Indeed this rich combination of disparate levels of meaning make the painting one of the acknowledged 15th-century masterpieces of Sienna, a great center of religion and art.

Charles Joseph Natoire, painting in France during the 18th century—a time when religious art was on the wane—is more literal and less awe inspiring in his depiction of *The Expulsion From Paradise*. Realizing that his academic colleagues would check their Bibles carefully for mistakes in his excursion into religious history painting, he even includes the usually neglected apron of fig leaves around Adam's waist. Like Giovanni di Paolo, he chooses a golden tone for the forbidden fruit and provides a host of angels for God's retinue. While his Almighty is painted according to the same conventions as Giovanni's, his Adam and Eve are unusually weepy and woebegone in their grief as they plead with

God for the right to stay in Eden. And unlike Giovanni he puts no intermediary between the couple and their maker. But the extraordinary beauty of Natoire's setting gives credence to Adam and Eve's sorrow; who would want to leave this lovely park?

The handsome ram between Adam and Eve is the unofficial mascot of French 18th-century rustic painting, so often does he appear in bucolic settings. A cow is also shown. And the serpent who brought all this trouble to humanity can be seen slithering off into the landscape. To the courtiers who patronized Natoire, idealized views such as this one were about as close as they ever got to rural life. Though the darling of their intellectual circle, the philosopher Jean-Jacques Rousseau, said "we never return to the times of innocence and equality, when we have once departed from them," paintings such as Natoire's provided French aristocrats with a vicarious means of escape from the stifling artifice of Louis XV's court. These ladies and gentlemen were so far removed from pristine nature, however, that they didn't realize the high degree of contrivance in such visions.

In addition to the other differences between these two paintings, they illustrate how an artist's choice of materials can impact the durability of his work over time: Giovanni di Paolo painted his scene on wood, and age has brought many hairline cracks to the work, all visible even in a reproduction. Natoire, however, painted his picture on copper, which binds pigment in such a way that the colors never fade or change and cracks never appear.

The Expulsion from Paradise
CHARLES JOSEPH NATOIRE, French, 1700–1777

Purchase, Mr. and Mrs. Frank E. Richardson III, George T. Delacorte, Jr., and Mr. and Mrs. Henry J. Heinz II Gifts; Victor Wilbour Memorial, Marquand and the Alfred N. Punnett Endowment Funds; and the Edward Joseph Gallagher Memorial Collection, Edward J. Gallagher, Jr. Bequest, 1987, The Metropolitan Museum of Art, New York. Oil on copper, 26 3/4 x 19 3/4 in.

Adam and Eve Mourning the Death of Abel
ELIHU VEDDER, American, 1836–1923

The Newark Museum, Gift of the American Academy of Arts
& Letters 1955. Oil on canvas, 14 1/4 x 47 1/4 in.

Adam and Eve Mourning

Cain, the farmer, and Abel, the shepherd, were the sons of Adam and Eve. Their births and deaths are recorded in Genesis, but nothing is known of their upbringing. The Holy Scripture does note that they brought the fruits of their labors to the Lord. Abel's offering pleased God, but Cain's did not. He was despondent and angry over this rejection, so God counseled him to do well and master the temptation to sin. In spite of this good advice, the jealous Cain killed his brother when they were alone in the fields. Shortly thereafter God asked him, "Where is Abel your brother?" and Cain rudely replied, "Am I my brother's keeper?" But God knew of Cain's evil deed and cursed him to a life of vagrancy. He also placed a mark on Cain to ward off those who might be tempted to murder one so disfavored. Thereafter Cain dwelt in the land east of Eden, where he eventually built the first city. If the brutish, cyclopedic altars attributed to him and his brother by Elihu Vedder in *Adam and Eve Mourning the Death of Abel* are any indication of his metropolis' architectural style, it must have been impressive.

According to the Holy Scriptures, Adam and Eve replaced Abel with a third son named Seth, but in art they wept first. Here Vedder shows the first parents in deep and dignified sorrow. Neither looks at the other, but their hands almost touch. Adam holds a scarf to his tear-stained face, and Eve is given the posture of a woman who is exhausted but collecting herself,

perhaps already contemplating a new life. Although the red top of her costume might look like a vamp's evening wear to the modern eye, and Adam's blue top like an undershirt, late 19th-century viewers would have seen these articles of clothing as plain, poor garments associated with peasants. The sickle near Adam's left foot would have belonged to Cain and might even have been the murder weapon.

During his long life, American expatriate Elihu Vedder witnessed the first flowering of a native American style of art, the Hudson River School of landscape painting. Affirmative and almost religious in its attitude toward nature, it was unsuited to the anxious and uncertain mood of the country after the Civil War. Of all the artists at work in the United States at the time, only Vedder's deeply psychological paintings reflected the traumatic era of Reconstruction. Because his contemporaries were puzzled by his style, Vedder moved to Rome in 1866, where he could find a more sophisticated environment in which to paint. In time, he returned home to create significant murals at Bowdoin College in Maine and at the Library of Congress in Washington, D.C. Among his most enduring creations, however, are his illustrations for a book of poetry, *The Rubáiyát of Omar Khayyám*.

The Deluge

Every ancient civilization tells the story of a massive flood that caused the end of mankind. Of particular interest to Biblical scholars are the tales of the Mesopotamians, Sumerians, and Babylonians, uneasy neighbors of the Israelites at various periods in their history. Each of these Semitic peoples included in their stories a universal human survivor who provided a bridge between the old, sinful world and the new, purified one.

In the Judeo-Christian Bible that survivor is Noah, who alone of all mankind found favor with God. Thus, when the Creator decided to destroy all of life, he chose to save Noah and his family and to put into their care one male and female of each animal species on earth. In order to house this vast menagerie during the deluge, Noah was instructed to build a three-decked boat or ark. After construction was complete and all the animals on board, the rains came, water covered the Earth, and God "blotted out every living thing that was upon the face of the ground" (Genesis 7:23).

Painters of many ages have been drawn to the story of the flood. In *The Deluge*, Hans Baldung Grien, one of Germany's greatest 16th-century artists, takes a very literal approach to the story. While he seems almost to delight in showing the agony of drowning and the grotesque postures of those hoping to avoid such a fate, his ark is a contrivance of unusual and even comical ingenuity. It looks like the top cabinet of a great grandfather clock, with a huge door instead of a face with dials and numerals. On the door is a massive padlock for, according to the Bible, the Lord locked Noah and his company into the ark. The door also features

ornamentation called *strapwork*, common in architecture and the decorative arts during Baldung's lifetime. Surrounding the storm-tossed vessel is a furious sky against which great streaks of lightning illuminate background details, while in the foreground figures appear pale against the turgid, opaque sea. Baldung's manipulation of light and dark causes the viewer's eyes to patrol every square inch of devastation. In so doing, one can spy the strongest humans trying to climb onto the ark. A plucky child imitates their endurance in the prow

of a rowboat in the lower right corner of the painting. There is weeping, lamenting, and perhaps even cursing, but there is no praying. Only those inside the ark have faith in God.

In around 1840, science attracted the innovative English artist J. M. W. Turner to the subject of the Great Flood. In *The Evening of the Deluge*, he addresses two topics of particular interest to his own age. First, he seeks to disprove the theories about color put forth by Johann Wolfgang von Goethe, the famous German writer, who

The Deluge

HANS BALDUNG GRIEN, German, 1484–1545

Historiches Museum, Bamberg, Germany. Oil on wood panel, 31 15/16 x 25 1/4 in.

assigned all colors values of "plus and minus." Turner pointedly uses blacks, acid yellows, and gray greens by themselves because Goethe said they could not succeed without the presence of their complements. Second, Turner turns to the subject of the deluge to explain the disappearance of prehistoric creatures whose fossilized remains had been the object of recent discovery. It amused and baffled the artist to contemplate their demise because they were not welcome on the ark. To make his point, he includes a long-extinct ichthyosaur (which looks rather like a crocodile) and sets him in the lower right portion of his painting, where he wistfully watches the procession of animals moving toward the distant boat.

Although the emerging modern sciences fascinated Turner, his personal vision was romantic, emotional, and subjective. While the most distinguished woman scientist of the day, the astronomer Mary Somerville, introduced him to her circle's arcane studies, it was her poetry that really inspired him. He even inscribed a poem by Somerville on the back of one of his deluge paintings. Describing the event as "the

darkening Deluge," the poet imagined, among other things, that "The roused birds forsook their nightly shelters screaming." Turner translated this image into a spiral of feathered creatures descending like a vortex from heaven to the ark. They alone reflect the terror that the rising tides in the lower central portion of the canvas portend, the same terror so graphically evident in the painting by Hans Baldung Grien.

In works like *The Evening of the Deluge*, Turner came close to inventing abstract art. His vision, however, was too spiritual, too focused on the idea of light as a generative force, and too concerned with the ultimate consequence of all things on earth for him to truly embrace the concept of pure abstraction. But only 15 years separate his death from the birth of Wassily Kandinsky, one of the pioneers of abstract art. From 1908 through 1913, Kandinsky produced series after series of paintings in which he systematically eliminated every representational element.

Three paintings exist by Kandinsky on the subject of the deluge. In the first, human bodies can be seen as they toss to and fro amid the gigantic waves. Although the artist adopts a closer vantage point, the painting is like Baldung's in character. The second version reduces the human beings to ghost-like shapes, and the water to broad slashing lines and softer cloud-like

forms. The final version, *Improvisation Deluge* of 1913, is the one reproduced here. In it Kandinsky sets aside all references to the biblical story, or any other narrative, and retains only the rhythms of the original composition. Colors are arbitrarily changed from those of water and flesh. Oval forms of pinks, yellows, and light blues seem to leap out from the deeper swirl of blues and blacks, with luminous, pastel stripes intercepting their movement. In terms of art theory, the painting is a celebration of color, line, and form. As a religious work, it is far more optimistic than the interpretations of Baldung and Turner. The artist himself insisted in the catalog of the second exhibition of the *Neue Kunstlervereinigung München* (Munich, 1910/11) that what he had created was "a new world," bearing the stamp of his personality and "springing from inner necessity." He spoke of "the materialization of spiritual values," which communicate "what is secret by what is secret."

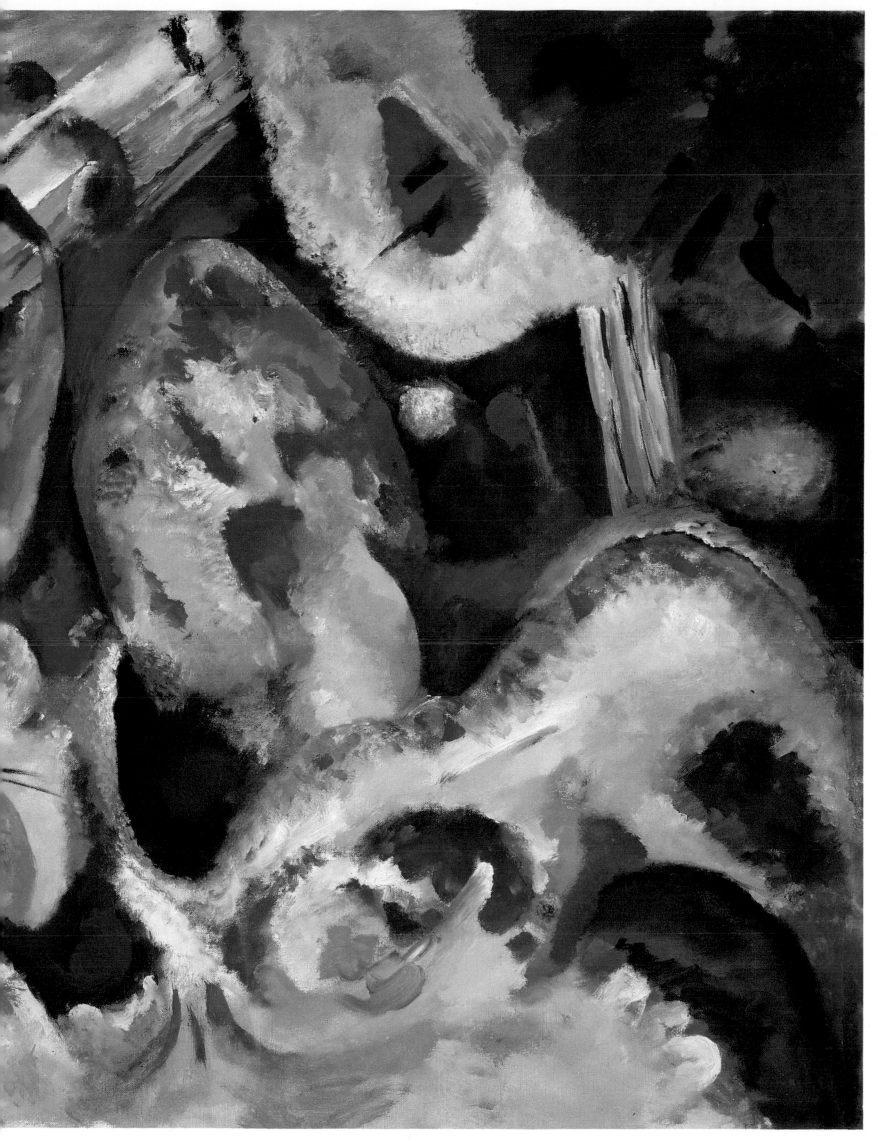

It rained for 40 days and 40 nights and, when the turbulent waters of the flood finally calmed, the ark and all of its inhabitants came to rest atop Mount Ararat. The ark can be seen in the background of the 17th-century Dutch painting *Animals from Noah's Ark* by Melchior de Hondecoeter. In actuality, Ararat is the highest and most inaccessible of the mountains of eastern Turkey, Armenia, and Kurdistan, and its rugged terrain would have created a virtually impossible descent for large animals like elephants and camels. The oldest Eastern accounts of the Great Flood do not mention Ararat, but only "the mountains of Kardu," among which are heights as comfortable as the one pictured by Melchior.

Appropriately, at the extreme left of the painting is a rooster, crowing his salutary greeting to a truly new day—the animals' first on land in ten months. But the peacock and crested crane misinterpret this raucous intrusion into the peace of their new home. They turn their heads to look for predators, behavior that perhaps they didn't have to exercise during the cramped stay on the boat. The dog in the right foreground makes it clear that something is approaching, but not from the direction in which the two exotic birds are looking. Hondecoeter apparently understood the psychology of these creatures—bird and mammal—and achieved sheer beauty in his execution of their anatomy, fur, and feathers.

Only a few of the animals are shown in pairs—as they entered the Ark—but among them are creatures that would have been familiar to Hondecoeter's audience, for the artist enjoyed enormous success as an animal painter and frequently repeated birds and beasts from one painting to another. Indeed, the cast of characters featured here performed in a large repertory of paintings. Most of them had their genesis in quick but realistic oil sketches created by the artist whenever he saw a new or exotic animal. He referred to these works throughout his long career.

Hondecoeter was familiar with the transport of animals by ship, for he often went to the docks of Amsterdam to paint creatures that sailors carried back to Holland from the Dutch East and West Indies. Like Noah's menagerie, they must have looked the worse for wear after their arduous voyages. But, in *Animals from Noah's Ark*, Hondecoeter ignores the likelihood of their poor condition and presents them in a pristine state, as though they were the beasts of Eden.

While many exotic animals reached Holland by means of its far-reaching fleet, most of the birds and animals shown here were already quite familiar to the Dutch during Hondecoeter's day, including the peacock, which was a major source of banquet food. Incidentally, patterns of animal habitation had changed drastically from ancient times to the time of Hondecoeter. For instance, archaeologists have demonstrated that elephants and rhinoceroses, now native only to Africa and southern Asia, were common in Mesopotamia during the Bronze Age.

Animals from Noah's Ark

MELCHIOR DE HONDECOETER, Dutch, 1636–1695

Herzog Anton-Ulrich-Museum, Brunswick, Germany. Oil on canvas, 63 $^{15}/_{16}$ x 84 1/2 in.

Noah Sacrificing After the Deluge
BENJAMIN WEST, American, 1738-1820
The San Antonio Museum Association. Oil on canvas,
72 x 138 in.

Noah Sacrificing

Of all the beings on earth, only Noah was righteous and found favor with God. If Benjamin West's interpretation of *Noah Sacrificing After the Deluge* can be trusted, then it would seem that Noah's three sons, Shem, Ham, and Japheth, experienced shipboard conversions during the deluge, for they appear here in deep prostration before the altar that their father built after descending from the ark. The women are, left to right, Noah's wife, full of fervor, and her three rather coy daughters-in-law. (Coyness was an 18th-century convention commonly used in the depiction of young women.)

The Bible says that God smelled the offerings that Noah burned, and was pleased. West, wisely, does not show us this sensory God, but he evokes the Almighty's presence by the doves alighting on the stone altar. In his massive orange-red cloak, which dominates the entire composition, Noah is a patriarch of noble strength. West shows his eyes as tiny orbs of light in dark pits, as though he enjoyed no sleep during the deluge. His hands, drawn with the brush as though it were a pen, and those of his wife, send thanks to the Almighty. Because of the low angle from which it is depicted, the altar is as much a focus of the painting as is Noah. And well it should be, because the Patriarch's offering elicited the promise from God that "While the earth remains, seed-time and harvest, cold and heat, summer and winter, day and night shall not cease" (Genesis 8:22).

West was an American Quaker who became famous during a long career in England. In paintings like this one, he introduced his adopted country to the Italian 18th-century style of the Tiepolos, the great family of painters who dominated Venetian art during the early part of West's lifetime and whose work the American obviously admired. *Noah Sacrificing* was executed with the royal taste in mind, for it was one of the decorations commissioned of West by George III for the chapel of Windsor Castle. The King, however, went mad, and the commission was withdrawn by his prosaic wife.

Patriarchs

The Meeting of Abraham and Melchizedek

One of the descendants of Noah through his son Shem was Abraham, to whom God promised his blessings and the prospects of a great nation (Genesis 12:2).

Lot, the nephew of this patriarch, was taken captive in a battle between five rulers of the Jordan plain and four invading Mesopotamian kings. With only 318 men, Abraham routed the armies of the invaders and rescued Lot and all of his possessions. After this victory, another of the region's city-kings, Melchizedek, who was also a priest, greeted Abraham with gifts of bread and wine, and blessed him in the name of "God Most High." For his part, Abraham offered the ruler-priest a tenth of his war booty. Although Melchizedek does not appear again in Genesis, his name is celebrated in the 110th Psalm, in which the coming messianic ruler is called "a priest forever after the order of Melchizedek" (Psalm 110:4). Accordingly, the old ruler-priest is viewed with considerable interest. Held as a heavenly judge by some, he is the subject of numerous sacred texts, including the Talmud, the Epistle to the Hebrews, and the writings of Josephus, the first-century A.D. Jewish historian. His importance derives, at least in part, from his domain, Salem, which was later Jerusalem. The Bible does not provide his lineage, so he is seen as that anomaly necessary for the establishment of a celibate clergy, an autogenerative priest.

In *The Meeting of Abraham and Melchizedek*, Rubens garbs Abraham in a chain mail skirt and a 17th-century cuirass, military armor that might at first glance seem foreign to his role as patriarch of the nation. He was,

The Meeting of Abraham and Melchizedek

PETER PAUL RUBENS, Flemish, 1577–1640

Gift of Syma Busiel, National Gallery of Art, Washington, D.C. Oil on wood panel, 26 x 32 ¹/₂ in.

PRECEDING PAGES

RUBENS: *Lot's Flight from Sodom*

(detail)

however, the chief of a large tribe of shepherds and cattlemen, and these men would have been required to answer his call to arms, if needed, as did the warriors who helped him free Lot. Melchizedek has a laurel wreath over his philosopher's cap, surely a humanist's conception of what so celebrated a character would wear.

Abraham takes the bread offered him by the priest-king as more loaves are passed to his soldiers in the background. Servants hoist ornate urns from a wine cellar, and one of them, struggling to carry a huge vessel up the stairs, glances at the viewer as if he fears that there will be more people to serve.

The festoons that surround the scene are like the ones that decorated entry arches and floats when important dignitaries came to visit Antwerp, the city in which Rubens lived. The great artist himself designed such tributes in 1635 for the arrival in Antwerp of their new viceroy, the Cardinal Infante Ferdinand. Rubens also had a triumphal arch permanently constructed at his home, separating his courtyard from his garden.

Painted on wood around 1625, *The Meeting of Abraham and Melchizedek* is only 26 inches wide, small in size for the flamboyant Rubens. While he ordinarily had many helpers assisting him with his paintings, this one is entirely by his own hand.

Abraham and the Three Angels

Abraham settled in Hebron, near Mamre, in the parched southern part of Judah, after decades of intermittent sojourns. His trek started from Ur, his Mesopotamian birthplace, and he later journeyed to Haran in the north, to Egypt in the south, and finally to the Negev. Mamre was a beloved spot to him, and he returned to it often. He even built an altar to God there. And it was at Mamre that he experienced a number of theophanies, the first of which is the subject of this painting.

It was a hot day, the Bible story says, when Abraham saw three men approaching his tent. Perhaps from his earlier conversations with God, he knew that they were angelic messengers. At any rate, he addressed them in the singular—as "Lord"—asked them to refresh themselves, and to rest a while. They agreed, and very quickly he had his wife, Sarah, baking cakes, and his servants roasting a calf. During the course of the meal, one of the men asked Abraham, "Where is Sarah your wife?" "In the tent," he replied. Then the man said "I will surely return to you in the spring, and Sarah your wife shall have a son" (Genesis 18:9–10). Sarah, who overheard this prophecy, was an old woman, far beyond the age of childbearing, and her husband was nearly 100 years old, so she laughed. The speaker heard her but repeated his prophecy. As the narration continues, it becomes clear that these are the words of the Lord himself.

Much of the biblical story of Abraham concerned the patriarch's preoccupation with his lack of an heir, for God's covenant with him was to be fulfilled through his children. Sarah suggested that he mate with her Egyptian maidservant, Hagar, and this he gladly did. From their union came a child, Ishmael, but with the visit of the three angels everything in the household of Abraham and Sarah changed.

Although the account in Genesis places the meeting between Abraham and the three angels under the oaks of Mamre, near the door to the patriarch's tent, Gaudenzio Ferrari's painting *Abraham and the Three Angels* stages this auspicious event in front of a house. An imaginary line following the stone wall in the center of the painting divides the composition into two segments. To the left of this line are the angels, representing the Holy Trinity to Italian viewers of the 16th century, and to the right are all the earthly beings, including Hagar and the infant Ishmael leaning on the wall. The posture of Abraham, who is bringing the roast to the table, and that of his wife, who is eavesdropping in the upper right, and the angle of the arm of the center angel reinforce the artist's emphasis on the diagonal. This compositional device represents a break from the rigid symmetry of the Renaissance and the onset of new forms that presage the Baroque, the style of the 17th century.

Abraham and the Three Angels
GAUDENZIO FERRARI, Italian, ca. 1471/81–1546
Location unknown.

Lot's Flight from Sodom

PETER PAUL RUBENS, Flemish, 1577–1640

John and Mabel Ringling Museum of Art, Sarasota, Florida. Oil on canvas, 85 ½ x 96 in.

Lot's Flight from Sodom

Two of the angels who visited Abraham went on to Sodom to see if that wicked city's sins were as great as they had heard. Lot, Abraham's nephew, invited them to spend the night at his home, but before they could take to bed, they and their host had to fight off the male population of the city because these evil men wanted to rape them. This incident was confirmation enough of Sodom's depravity. Hence the angels told their host to flee the city with his family because they were going to destroy Sodom the next day.

In *Lot's Flight from Sodom*, Peter Paul Rubens shows Lot and his family hurrying out of the city under the guidance of one of the angels. Lot looks back as he tries to convince the husband of one of his daughters to join them. The young man refuses, believing that Lot was just jesting about Sodom's fate.

Rubens dwells on the human side of the story, rather than on its moral lessons and the opportunity it provides for virtuoso displays of destruction. He shows the fire and smoke of the city in the background, but his emphasis is on Lot's family. Lot's wife, immediately behind her husband, is weeping. Even though there is not one righteous neighbor in the entire city, the departure from everything familiar is wrenching to her. The angel has warned them, "Flee for your life; do not look back" (Genesis 19:17), but she will ignore this command; as a consequence, she will turn into a pillar of salt. This harsh fate is foreshadowed in the gray column against which Rubens poses his figures.

The daughters of Lot are also deeply saddened by their departure. Both have left behind their husbands and their kinfolk, all soon to die in the fire and brimstone rained down upon that doomed city.

In one of the few instances in the Old Testament where God turned his face away from the sins of the people of Abraham, or at least their near kin, Lot's daughters committed incest with their father. Isolated from all other human beings and living in a cave, the girls convinced themselves that, in order to preserve the family line, they must trick their aged parent into having intercourse with them by getting him senselessly drunk. First came the eldest daughter. Lot was so tipsy he did not know it was she "when she lay down or when she arose" from his bed (Genesis 19:33). The next night the same performance was repeated by the younger daughter, who in the painting holds a mirror but turns from her reflection. The two male children that sprang from these inter-familial relations became the patriarchs of the Moabites and the Ammonites, neighbors and often enemies of Israel.

In Bonifazio de' Pitati's colorful and disturbing painting *Lot and His Daughters*, one of the young ladies is seen plying Lot with wine, a beverage that he seems to enjoy. Her bright red dress is disheveled and she is barefoot as she tries to excite her father. Sodom burns in the background as diagonal sheets of brimstone rain down on it. The family's flight from that city of sin can be seen on the broad road to their mountain home. Two putti (the Italian word for the children who appear in paintings as allegorical creatures or little wingless angels) appear behind the younger daughter, one of them wearing a mask. The mirror and the mask bring a didactic tone to the painting.

Inspired by ancient Greek and Roman models, the Renaissance scholars of Bonifazio's day codified a complex iconography to illustrate certain human traits and characteristics. The Latin terms for these qualities became as well known among intellectuals as their vernacular names. The mirror was a symbol of prudence and wisdom, while ideas of truth and falsehood were alluded to by the mask. The daughters of Lot, therefore, act out the struggle between *voluptas* (carnal pleasure) and *virtus* (goodness or virtue). Pictures illustrating this particular and very enduring human struggle were very rarely seen by the common people of the day. Rather, these works were kept in the private chambers of the wealthy, usually near their bedrooms. While they were ostensibly retained as moralistic lessons, the titillating aspects of these sexy pictures did them no harm with collectors. In *Lot and His Daughters*, Bonifazio's use of the mask must have had a special appeal for his fellow Venetians, because they were accustomed to donning elaborate facial ornamentation during the annual *carnevale* festivities, events which were known for their license and drunkenness.

Lot and His Daughters
BONIFAZIO DE' PITATI, Italian, 1487–1553
The Chrysler Museum, Norfolk, Virginia. Oil on canvas,
48 1/2 x 65 5/8 in.

Abraham Turning Away Hagar

Just as the angelic visitor predicted, Sarah bore Abraham a son, whom his parents called Isaac, from the Hebrew for "laughter." When the child was weaned, Abraham gave a great feast, and on that day Sarah decided that the patriarch had to forsake his concubine, Hagar, and her child, Ishmael, "for he shall not be heir with my son Isaac" (Genesis 21:10). Abraham had grown fond of the boy, but God told Abraham that if he did as Sarah demanded, he would "make a nation of the son of the slave woman" (Genesis 21:13).

Ishmael had already passed his 13th year—the age of manhood in the Jewish religion—when these events transpired, but the Biblical accounts refer to him as a "lad" and he is always pictured as such by artists. In *Abraham Turning Away Hagar*, Emile-Jean-Horace Vernet follows this tradition, but he gets all of the other details exactly as the Bible described them. Long, dark shadows of the early morning are cast by the dunes, the tent, and the figures in the foreground. Almost hidden are Sarah and young Isaac, she staring out from the shadows of the tent at her husband, the child asleep on her lap. Sheep are corralled within the oasis, for Abraham's wealth lay primarily in his flocks. The patriarch wears the garb of a Bedouin chieftain, while Hagar is modestly dressed as an Arab woman except that her arm and part of her right breast are exposed, a reminder of her low status as a slave.

Vernet has chosen to depict the moment at which Abraham sends Hagar and Ishmael on their way. Stony faced, he points in the direction of the desert, and gently pushes his son from him. Hagar appears hurt, furious, and obedient all at the same time. As for Ishmael, one can see in him the potential to become what God told Hagar he would be: "a wild ass of a man, his hand against every man and every man's hand against him" (Genesis 16:12). Note his stance. Although he grasps his mother's skirt, surprised by his father's command, his legs are not set to move.

Abraham Turning Away Hagar
ÉMILE-JEAN-HORACE VERNET, French, 1789–1863
Musée des Beaux-Arts, Nantes, France. Oil on canvas, 31 15/16 x 25 1/16 in.

Hagar and Ishmael

Hagar and Ishmael nearly died in the desert after Abraham banished them from his household. According to Genesis, Hagar put her son under a bush when their water was gone, and walked the distance of a bow shot so that she would not have to watch his death. They were saved by God, who heard the boy's cries, and produced a well of water to quench their thirst. He also sent an angel, who prophesied that Ishmael's heirs would form a great nation.

Genesis' account of this story is more descriptive but less dramatic than Jean-Francois Millet's painting of 1849. The artist neglects the bush under which the mother placed the lad, and gives neither figure relief from the sun. With the empty water skin between them, they both are dying on the dunes. Ishmael's body is strewn across a rise in the sand, and, as he moans pathetically, he finds the strength to bring his arm to his mouth, perhaps to touch his tongue to a bead of perspiration. His mother cries out, unable to watch his agony, her body rigid from the strain of being unable to aid him.

Pietro da Cortona's painting *Hagar and the Angel* stands in marked contrast to Millet's version of the story. Instead of depicting the mother and child in agony, he shows the pair after their rescue. The desert has become a flourishing forest, and the two wanderers are healthy, beautiful beings. Her troubles forgotten, Hagar converses with the gorgeous angel while Ishmael looks on, frightened either by the heavenly apparition or by the news of his future role in history, or both.

Cortona focuses the viewer's eye on the exchange between the angel and Hagar by selecting for their costumes the lightest colors on the canvas. They are presented as ideal beauties, with Hagar's elegant proportions and youthful figure particularly emphasized. Indeed she is seen less as a mother than an object of desire engaged in a flirtation with an angel.

Millet, on the other hand, eliminates color altogether and concentrates on the

Hagar and the Angel
PIETRO DA CORTONA, Italian, 1596–1669
The John and Mabel Ringling Museum of Art, Sarasota, Florida. Oil on canvas, 45 x 58 ¹³/₁₆ in.

outlines of the two figures. From such a
rendering, one can understand why the
Impressionists and Post-Impressionists of
the next generation, including Vincent van
Gogh, greatly admired his drawings. It is a
style that reduces a story to its most
human and tragic components. It is said
that he witnessed thirst, starvation, and
death during a cholera epidemic, which
occurred during the very year in which he
painted this moving scene. He was not
known to make drawings from life, so his
evocation of agony would have come from
his deeply felt, internalized remembrances.

According to the Bible, Ishmael became
an expert bowman; he continued to live in
the desert for the rest of his life, marrying
an Egyptian woman selected by his mother
and fathering her children. He returned
only once to his homeland, and that was
for his father's burial. Both Moslems and
Jews regard him as the first patriarch of the
desert tribes, and Arabs venerate him as
their forefather, whose most famous offspring was Mohammad. In Christian theology, however, Ishmaelite is the name given
an outcast. St. Paul, in the New Testament, uses the story of Hagar and her son
to show that it is better to be the child of a
free woman than the offspring of a slave.
Clearly, artists of the Christian era were
not drawn to this tale for its theological
lessons, nor because they wished to trace
the ancestry of the Bedouins. Rather, they
were attracted by the romance and ensuing
tragedy of the beautiful Hagar.

Jean-François Millet, called a socialist by
his critics, and Pietro da Cortona, the decorator of great Baroque churches, are separated in time by two centuries, but in spirit
they are much further apart. The subject of
Hagar and Ishmael is their sole meeting
point. Millet was commissioned by the
government, quite early in his career, to
paint the subject as a mural decoration. It
was his only venture into official art and it
was never delivered or exhibited. Cortona,
on the other hand, spent his entire life as
an official painter of murals. *Hagar and the
Angel* is one of his rare easel paintings.

Hagar and Ishmael
JEAN-FRANÇOIS MILLET, French, 1814–1875
Rijksmuseum H.W. Mesdag, The Hague. Oil on canvas, 57 1/8 x 91 3/4 in.

The Sacrifice of Issac

To test Abraham's devotion, God ordered the patriarch to journey three days from his home in Beersheba and there, on a mountaintop, to sacrifice his son, Isaac, as a burnt offering. Abraham obediently took Isaac on the journey, but, as he prepared the site for sacrifice, Isaac asked him, "Where is the lamb for the burnt offering?" "God will provide himself the lamb," Abraham replied (Genesis 22:7–8). He then bound his son and placed him on top of a wooden pyre, but before he could complete the ritual slaughter, an angel from heaven stopped him, saying "I know that you fear God for you have not withheld your son, your only son, from me." He then provided a ram for the offering.

Both Abraham and Isaac are remarkably passive in this story, with the father submitting to the will of God, and the son quiescent to the wishes of his father. Yet the story is still moving. Given Abraham's long-standing wish for an heir, someone who could fulfill his covenant with God in the wake of his wife's barrenness, his willingness to sacrifice Isaac becomes a drama of epic proportions. His compliance is even more saddening when one remembers that he banished his other son, Ishmael, also at God's command. The New Testament writer of *The Letter to the Hebrews* states that Abraham was obedient because he believed that the Lord would restore his son to life, but there is no indication of such an expectation in the Old Testament.

The Sacrifice of Isaac is the most frequently painted incident in Abraham's life, and the version chosen for this volume is by the 18th-century Italian master, Giandomenico Tiepolo. In this work Abraham appears to be in a daze, as if he has numbed himself to the awful consequences of the act he is about to perform. Frozen an instant before thrusting the silvery blade into the body of his son, he takes the news of the reprieve with surprise and incomprehension.

Indeed, he almost falls backward as God's messenger commands him to stop, pointing to the substitute sacrifice which is out of the picture plane. The artist adds a touch of mercy to the moment, one not mentioned in the Holy Scriptures—the blindfold over Isaac's eyes, held lovingly in place by Abraham's strong left hand.

The Sacrifice of Isaac is notable for its spare use of color and for the introduction of a number of symbols that would have been understood by Tiepolo's contemporaries. For example, the bright red robe that frames Isaac's near-naked body is the color of blood. Long associated with martyrdom in art, red was also the color of church vestments on days honoring martyred saints. The white cloth cinched around the lad's waist stands for purity. Tiepolo, known for his profuse use of color, uncharacteristically avoids bright hues for the angel's attire. Instead he cloaks the messenger of God in gray, thus keeping the viewer's focus on the young Isaac. Even the fluffy cloud under the angel leans toward the youth. Though the lad is positioned on the right side of the canvas, Tiepolo clearly makes him the main figure of this large and imposing painting.

The Sacrifice of Isaac
GIOVANNI DOMENICO TIEPOLO, Italian, 1727–1804
Purchase 1871, The Metropolitan Museum of Art, New York.
Oil on canvas, 15 ³/₄ x 21 in.

Abraham wanted his son Isaac to marry a woman from his homeland in northern Mesopotamia rather than someone from Canaan, his adopted land, so he sent his most trusted servant to search for such a young woman. When the functionary arrived in Nahor, the ancestral home of his master, it was evening, "the time when women go out to draw water" (Genesis 24:11). The old man devised a plan for finding Isaac's bride: the first single woman to offer water to his camels would be the chosen one. Immediately thereafter a beautiful young woman came to the well. Her name was Rebecca, and when she offered nourishment to the servant's beasts, the old man knew that he had found Abraham's daughter-in-law.

Two Venetian artists, separated in time by 125 years, selected moments of quiet drama for their paintings of *Rebecca at the Well*. Giovanni Antonio Pellegrini chose the biblical verses that described Rebecca as "very fair to look upon" and a virgin (Genesis 24:16), and the servant as gazing "at her in silence to learn whether the Lord had prospered his journey or not" (Genesis 24:21). Pellegrini assumed that Rebecca was surprised by the old man's attention, and he keeps her hair and costume unruffled despite the strenuous task of raising enough water for ten thirsty camels.

Paolo Veronese, the earlier and greater of the two artists, selected the next episode of the story for his depiction. The old servant has just given the maiden two gold bracelets. She caresses one of the heavy ornaments—they weighed 10 shekels, or roughly 5 pounds—while she looks suspiciously at the donor. There is also a hint of pleasure in her face. It is easy to imagine this woman conniving later in life to win the major portion of the family inheritance for her favorite son, Jacob. Veronese also convinces the viewer that she is hearty enough to draw heavy copper buckets full of water from a deep well and shrewd enough not to make a mistake about marriage.

The wealthy merchants of Venice provided artists with a constant stream of commissions as they tried to fill their palaces with colorful pictures. In Veronese's day, canvas replaced planks of wood as the surface of choice for painting. Lighter in weight, easier to transport, far less costly and faster to prepare than wood, stretched canvas enabled the Venetians to become the first artists in history to specialize in huge portable pictures. Many of these works ended up placed high on the walls of large rooms and even on ceilings. The low vantage point in both the Veronese and Pellegrini compositions suggests that the artists knew they would hang above eye level before creating them.

The two pictures have so many points in common that it is tempting to imagine Pellegrini looking at the Veronese painting while creating his own version of the story.

Both artists conceive the trusted servant of Abraham as bald and bearded, and of Rebecca as blond, with her hair gathered up in the back of her head. The white sleeves of her blouse in the Veronese painting are echoed not only in Pellegrini's treatment of the maiden's costume but also in the garb of the servant. Pellegrini, however, is far more decorative in his approach to the story than is Veronese. The latter shows utilitarian buckets and a deep well for the fetching of water, while the former introduces a carved spigot and an ornamented alabaster jug. Moreover, Veronese sets his characters against a dark backdrop in keeping with the biblical setting of early evening, while his compatriate prefers an altogether lighter palette. The love of pastel tones in 18th-century Venice led to an international style called Rococo, and Pellegrini brought this light-filled manner of painting to Austria, Germany, France, the Netherlands, and England, countries where he worked. Veronese, by contrast, spent most of his life in Venice. Nonetheless, his vast output influenced not only the artists of his own age but also those of Pellegrini's.

Rebecca at the Well
GIOVANNI ANTONIO PELLEGRINI, Italian, 1675–1741
The National Gallery, London. Oil on canvas,
50 1/8 x 41 1/8 in.

FOLLOWING PAGES
Rebecca at the Well
PAOLO VERONESE, Italian, 1528–1588
Samuel H. Kress Collection, National Gallery of Art,
Washington, D.C. Oil on canvas, 57 1/4 x 111 1/4 in.

The Marriage of Isaac and Rebecca

The Book of Genesis reported the marriage of Isaac and Rebecca in a few simple and tender words. Isaac took the maiden into his tent, "and she became his wife; and he loved her" (Genesis 24:67). But the great 18th-century French painter Claude Lorrain, in his *Landscape with the Marriage of Isaac and Rebecca*, sees to it that they had a party afterward. And it is a merry affair indeed. The couple dance for one another with timbrals in their hands. A melody comes from the flute and recorder of two young women on the left side of the picture. Ewers and platters of refreshments stand near the central figures in a quiet still life. And a servant far back on the edge of the grassy field pours wine. The guests are the groom's friends and their children, as well as the servants who accompanied Rebecca from her home far away.

Claude's Bible characters appear in his paintings primarily to justify the artist's passion for creating landscapes, which he produced one after another throughout his long career. In his day, serious painters were expected to dedicate themselves to the depiction of history, considered the highest form of art, and not waste their time copying nature. But Claude idealized what he saw in his surroundings, and his work found a ready and enthusiastic audience which regarded him as the great poet of Classical harmony. Indeed, his landscapes are restful, soothing, and in their focus on the horizon, even uplifting. This one also manages to evoke a sense of celebration as one of the great marriages of biblical history begins.

Rather than create a Middle East backdrop, Claude chose to set his scene in the Roman Campagna, an area that he loved and immortalized in many of his works. Clear evening light reveals a river spilling into a broad basin next to a mill with a

high tower. Claude decides against a colorful sunset for this occasion and creates instead a blue sky with only a narrow white band at the horizon and a few grayish white clouds above the celebrants. The setting sun itself is hidden behind the towering elm on the right.

The 19th-century landscape painter Jean-Baptiste Camille Corot so loved this picture that he borrowed its principal figures—Isaac, Rebecca, and their party—and relocated them to the Bay of Naples, a setting that also figured prominently in Claude's oeuvre. This painting's impact on Corot is only one instance of Claude's enormous influence on later generations of artists.

Landscape with the Marriage of Isaac and Rebecca

CLAUDE LORRAIN (Claude Gelée), French, 1600–1682

The National Gallery, London. Oil on canvas, 58 3/4 x 77 1/8 in.

Rebecca was barren, but Isaac pleaded with God to grant him children and shortly thereafter she conceived twins. According to the Bible, "the children struggled together within her," because "the one shall be stronger than the other, the elder shall serve the younger" (Genesis 25:23). The first to emerge from the womb was Esau, whose heel was in the grip of the second child, Jacob (whose name was later changed to Israel).

Esau was a hunter and the favorite of his father, while Jacob, a shepherd, was his mother's pet. The most critical moment in their struggle against one another came when their old father asked Esau to kill and prepare for him the "savory food, such as I love." It was to be a symbolic meal, binding the two men, after which Isaac would bless his elder son. Overhearing the instructions, Rebecca summoned Jacob, and, upon Esau's departure for the hunt, had her favorite kill and cook two kids and serve them to his father. To fool Isaac into thinking that he was his twin, "Rebecca took the best garments of Esau . . . and put them on Jacob . . . and the skins of the kids she put upon his hands and upon the smooth part of his neck," for—unlike Jacob—Esau was hairy. Isaac was fooled. Then Esau returned with his meal and he realized the deception. "Your brother came with guile," he told Esau ruefully, "and he has taken away your blessing" (Genesis 27:3–35).

The moment of deception is often shown in art, but strangely Esau is much neglected. In 1859, the great French mural painter Pierre Puvis de Chavannes redressed this oversight somewhat with his noble and energy-filled painting *[Esau's] Return from the Hunt.* A pagan quality fills this work, especially in Esau's tigerskin cowl and the boar's head insignia on his lance. The two nearly naked youths who attend the hunter add a primal essence to the work, while the panting dogs add excitement and a rush of forward movement.

Hunting was a favorite pastime of the French aristocracy, one exclusively reserved for the nobility. By the mid-19th century, however, the rich middle class had mastered the etiquette associated with the sport and could well afford the horses, hounds, and riding habits that largely distinguished it from the lower class' pragmatic need to kill animals for food. Hunting scenes and paintings of the trophies of the hunt—artistically arranged piles of carcasses—were regularly used to decorate the dining rooms of the wealthy.

Pierre Puvis de Chavannes first turned to the subject in 1854 as part of a series of murals for the dining room of his brother's new house, depicting Bible stories involving meat, fish, bread, and wine. He repeated the Esau scene five years later and entered it into the Salon, the official exhibition of the Academy of Art. While his paintings had regularly been refused since 1850, this work was accepted. Perhaps its subject—hunting—struck a chord of French chauvinism. Thinking back to painting the scene in his brother's house, he later commented, "Ah, that day I knew I was going to be able to do what I wanted." Indeed, mural painting became his mission from then on, and he is ranked with the greatest muralists of all time.

[Esau's] Return from the Hunt
PIERRE PUVIS DE CHAVANNES, French, 1824–1898
Musée des Beaux-Arts, Marseilles. Oil on canvas,
135 ³/₄ x 116 ⁵/₈ in.

Jacob's Dream

Though Esau was the firstborn, he sold his birthright to Jacob. Isaac's blessing on the younger son—bestowed on him through his mother's trickery—further confirmed his future as family patriarch. Realizing that he was now son number two, Esau decided to murder his twin as soon as his father died. Rebecca discerned Esau's intentions, however, and sent Jacob out of harm's way to find a wife.

On his journey, the youth stopped to sleep, using a stone as a pillow, just as the Dutch painter Frans van Mieris I shows in *Jacob's Dream*. The artist also depicts what Jacob saw in his dream. "There was a ladder . . . to heaven" with angels ascending and descending it. God himself appeared at the top of the ladder and spoke to Jacob, promising the youth the land he slept on and a multitude of descendants who would be a blessing to the families of the Earth. "I am with you and will keep you wherever you go, and will bring you back to this land," God said. When Jacob arose, he was afraid. "How awesome is this place!" he exclaimed. "This is none other than the house of God, and this is the gate of heaven." Then he consecrated the place and called it *Bethel*, which is Hebrew for *House of God* (Genesis 28:10–19).

The Bible did not interpret Jacob's dream, but clearly God's blessing can be seen as further assurance of the lad's future as family patriarch despite Esau's seniority. Perhaps the ladder represented a symbol of difficulties overcome, meaning that the enmity between Esau and Jacob would be bridged.

Frans van Mieris I specialized in tiny pictures of interior scenes full of lively people. This exceptional miniature is a rare excursion for him into a biblical subject, and it is an unusually quiet picture compared to most of his output. Though Jacob's dream is shown in finely painted, pale tones in the left background, the sleeping, nearly naked youth is the artist's primary focus. Posed against a backdrop of dark shrubbery, the ivory flesh of Jacob's body reflects the heavenly light of the vision. The angels do not awaken him, but he lifts his right leg and moves his arms behind his head in a restless response to the message from God.

Jacob's Dream
FRANS VAN MIERIS I, Dutch, 1635–1681
Rijksmuseum, Amsterdam. Oil on wood panel,
8 1/2 x 11 1/2 in.

Jacob and Rachel at the Well

MASTER OF THE TWELVE APOSTLES, Italian, active first half of the 16th century

Collection of Piero Corsini, New York. Oil on canvas, 38 ³/₄ x 54 ¹/₈ in.

Jacob and Rachel at the Well

Rebecca sent her son Jacob to woo and wed one of the daughters of his uncle Laban. As soon as the youth arrived in Mesopotamia, where Laban lived, he met Rachel, the younger of his two female cousins, who was bringing her father's sheep to water at the well. They fell in love at once; to win Rachel's hand he agreed to work for her father for seven years. At the end of that time, however, Laban tricked him into marrying his eldest daughter, Leah, instead. For Rachel, Jacob had to labor another seven years.

Both the 16th-century Master of the

Twelve Apostles and his famous contemporary Paolo Veronese depict the moment of Jacob and Rachel's meeting. The men in the latter's painting are oblivious to Rachel's flirtations, but those of the anonymous Master realize that the young man and young woman have fallen in love. The man on the left might represent Laban, shrewdly figuring out how to exact seven years of labor from his husky relative in return for the promise of Rachel's hand.

The Italian Master of the Twelve Apostles works in a clearly focused style that was probably inspired by German artists living in Italy. The speckled and spotted goats play a later role in the narrative as

part of Jacob's wages for his second seven years of labor, and the bird, about to pounce on the snake, might be a comment on Laban's strategy. All of the other details are the artist's invention. They include in the lower left corner a double reed bag pipe, the instrument of the shepherds, and the neck of a cittern, a popular guitar-like instrument of the 16th century, which is propped against a branch behind the man thought to be Laban. Scholars have compared the features of this man to those of the famous Prince Leonello d'Este (1407–1450), so it is thought that this

Jacob and Rachel at the Well
PAOLO VERONESE, Italian, 1528–1588
Collection of Piero Corsini, New York. Oil on canvas,
32 $7/_8$ x 42 $1/_8$ in.

painting, created more than 50 years after the prince's death, might have been commissioned by one of Leonello's heirs to honor his acumen and musicality.

Veronese shows both sisters, Rachel seductively washing her feet at a masonry basin, with Leah peering over her back to examine the muscles in Jacob's bare leg. While the anonymous Master's Jacob shyly steals a look at Rachel, Veronese's young man is lost in his work. So too are the shepherds who help Rachel with her flock of white sheep and goats. Two dogs are included in both paintings. They symbolize the marital fidelity of Jacob's wives.

Veronese also adds an engaging camel, which was often included in Old Testament inventories to demonstrate a man's worth. Some writers suggest that the beast's face is a caricature of the artist. If so, it is one of the more amusing self-portraits in the history of art.

Jacob Wrestling with the Angel

In *Jacob Wrestling with the Angel*, the French Post-Impressionist artist Paul Gauguin seems to see the match as a vision. The Bible, however, presented it as an actual struggle, and every artist who pictured it before the 19th century took it literally.

It happened the night before Jacob was to be reunited with his twin, Esau. Worried about the impending meeting, Jacob went off to be alone. In his solitude, he encountered an unidentified man who engaged him in a wrestling match that consumed the entire night. When day came and Jacob was still fighting tirelessly, the man put the Hebrew's thigh out of joint and then asked to be released. "I will not let you go unless you bless me," Jacob responded. The man asked his tenacious opponent's name, and when he heard it, said "Your name shall no more be called Jacob, but Israel, for you have striven with God and with men, and have prevailed." After the man departed, Jacob concluded that, "I have seen God face to face, and yet my life is preserved" (Genesis 32:24–30). Gauguin interprets the "man" of the story to be an angel, as most artists did, and shows him at the moment that he "touched the hollow of (Jacob's) thigh" (Genesis 32:25).

Gauguin was deeply impressed by the simple faith of the peasants near Pont-Aven on the Bay of Biscay in Brittany, where he went to study painting early in his career as an artist. In *Jacob Wrestling with the Angel*, the struggle is witnessed by a group of Breton women on their way home from church. Though the ranking of spectators close to the viewer suggests a realistic situation, none of the figures cast shadows. The blood-red ground beneath the wrestlers is a second clue that the painting is more symbolic than real. Gauguin referred to this work as *The Vision after the Sermon, or Jacob and the Angel* suggesting perhaps that for the pious Breton women a Bible story, powerfully told, could be as real as life.

Gauguin was an innovator in art. He associated himself with many of the avant-garde artists of his day but outpaced them all in breaking with Impressionism and creating a new style of bold, flat patterns and pure colors to capture expressive and symbolic ideas. During his formative years at Pont-Aven, he quickly picked up innovations from anyone who had something to teach him. The very palette he favored in *Jacob and the Angel* had just been used hours earlier by Emil Bernard, a young friend of Gauguin, to demonstrate a particular way of separating colors with bold black lines. Gauguin not only learned the lesson but created a masterpiece.

Vision After the Sermon (Jacob Wrestling with the Angel)
PAUL GAUGUIN, French, 1848–1903
The National Gallery of Scotland, Edinburgh. Oil on canvas, 29 1/4 x 36 5/8 in.

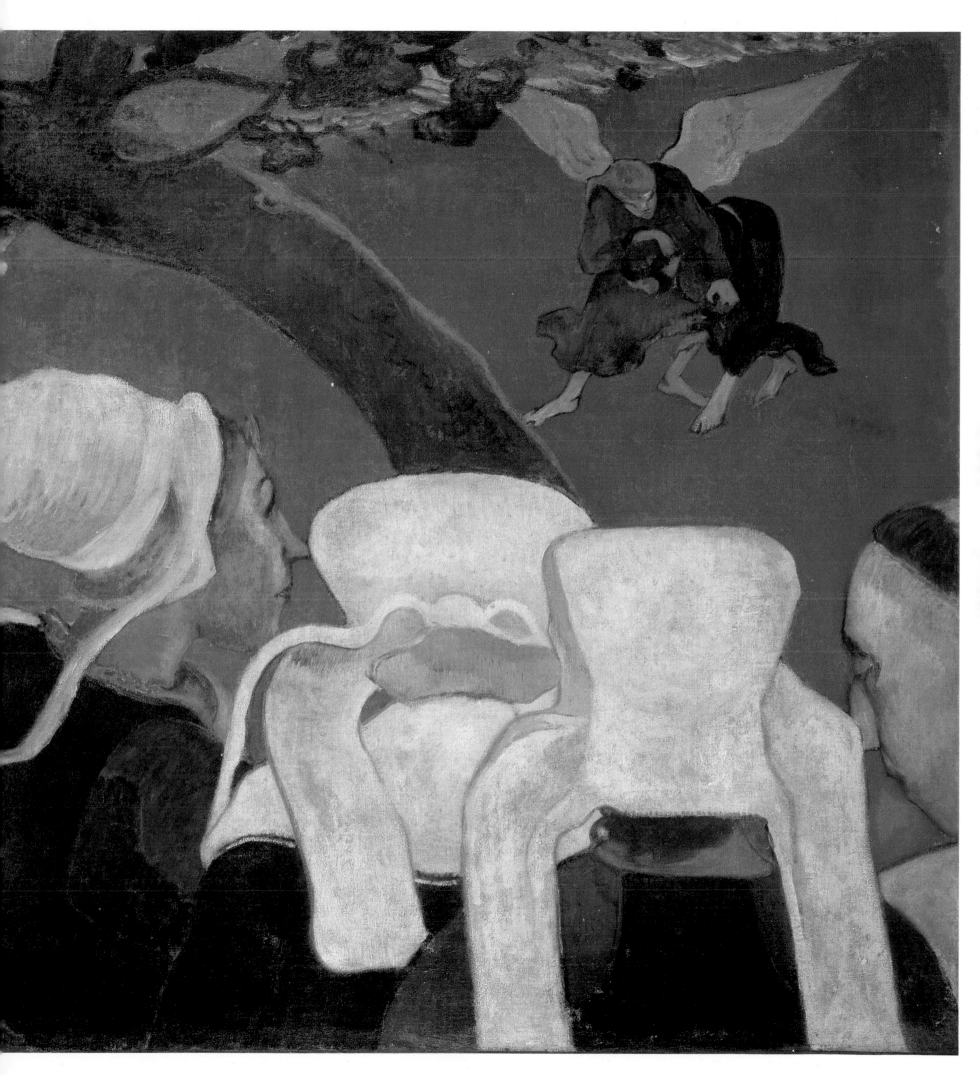

Jacob Asks Forgiveness of Esau

Jacob asked for a meeting between himself and his brother Esau, whom he had not seen since he had stolen his twin's inheritance in their youth. When he learned that Esau was en route with an armed band of 400 men, he began to fear that his brother would use the occasion to do him harm. To protect his holdings, Jacob cleverly concealed half of what he owned and arranged an extravagant gift for Esau: "Two hundred she-goats and twenty he-goats, two hundred ewes and twenty rams, thirty milch camels and their colts, forty cows and ten bulls, twenty she-asses and ten he-asses" (Genesis 32:14–15). They were sent out, one drove at a time, as his brother approached the place where Jacob waited, the idea being that by the time he and Esau met, his twin would be so overwhelmed by his generosity that the past would be forgotten. Even so, Jacob was nervous until the moment of Esau's arrival. Still he lined up his family for the reunion. Closest to him he put the family maids with their children; then Leah, his first wife, with their four children; and, finally, his beloved second wife, Rachel, and their son, Joseph. As it turned out, his fears proved groundless. Esau sought no revenge.

The moment of the brothers' meeting is pictured by Jan Victors in his masterpiece, *Jacob Seeking Forgiveness of Esau.* Jacob had wrestled with the angel the night before, so he was lame, but with the help of a walking stick he greeted his brother, "bowing himself to the ground seven times" (Genesis 33:3). According to the biblical narrative, Esau ran to meet him, but this is not shown by Jan Victors. His Esau is outside the picture frame and Jacob's eyes are directed at him, as are those of Leah from her camel mount under the shade of the great oriental umbrella. Very quickly, it becomes apparent that the *viewer* is Esau.

There was a convention in art, often used in the depiction of group scenes from history, that one member of the assemblage look directly at the viewer. This device personalized the action and more directly engaged anyone looking at the painting. Usually the character who looked out was one of the scene's lesser personages; sometimes he was even an anonymous bystander. Frequently he stood close to the picture frame, as though inviting the viewer to actually step into the painting and be a quiet witness to the action. Jan Victors, in *Jacob Seeking Forgiveness of Esau,* has expanded this convention to make the viewer a major participant in the scene by giving him Esau's vantage point. This clever artist may well have been inspired to paint Old Testament scenes by the example of his teacher, Rembrandt.

Jacob Seeking Forgiveness of Esau
JAN VICTORS, Dutch, 1619–1676
Martha Delzell Memorial Fund, Indianapolis Museum of Art.
Oil on canvas, 70 1/4 x 81 1/2 in.

Joseph was Jacob's 11th son but the first by the patriarch's most beloved wife, Rachel. He was disliked by his older siblings, for he was Jacob's favorite, the child of his old age. He also unwisely told his brothers of two prophetic dreams he'd had in which they bowed down to him. Moreover, he was the beneficiary of a marvelous coat, made for him by his father. It was a long coat "of many colors" with long sleeves. Only princes and scholars wore such fancy clothes, for laborers could not afford them, and anyway the sleeves would have interfered with their work. After he got this fine gift, Joseph's brothers—who were simple shepherds—hated him even more.

One day Jacob asked Joseph to go and see how his brothers were faring with their large flocks. The errand took him a long way from home. When his brothers saw Joseph coming, they decided to take revenge on him. At first they considered killing him then and there, but instead decided to leave him in a deep pit where they hoped a wild beast would finish him off. His fabled coat was dipped in the blood of a goat and brought back to Jacob as proof of his demise. Later, they changed their minds again and sold him as a slave to Ishmaelite traders, descendants of Abraham's first son, who bought him for 20 shekels and took him to Egypt.

In *Jacob Receiving Joseph's Blood-Stained Coat* by Diego Velázquez, a delegation of the brothers presents the soiled garment to the old patriarch. He recognizes it and exclaims "a wild beast has devoured him; Joseph is without doubt torn to pieces" (Genesis 37:33). One son has his bare back to the viewer, and shields his eyes from the bloody sight. Perhaps he is the eldest, Reuben, who prevented the others from killing Joseph and who was distressed by the boy's fate. The two who hold the coat are either genuinely saddened by their father's response or ingenuous actors. In the shadowy figures of the other two brothers, one senses the strain of keeping a "straight face."

In a number of royal portraits, which he painted later in his life, Velázquez used dogs, like the one here, as a decorative accessory. This canine, however, is not merely for show. He recognizes Joseph's scent on the coat, as well as that of the dead animal. Confused and angry, his noisy barks are intended to call the clan to action. But the patriarch pays him no mind, for he accepts his sons' lies.

This is one of the few pictures that Velázquez painted without a royal commission. The brilliantly successful artist was only 31 years of age at the time, and had been chief painter to King Philip IV of Spain for close to seven years. At the urging of the Flemish master, Peter Paul Rubens, who had recently visited Madrid on a diplomatic mission, Velázquez journeyed to Rome, where he executed this canvas and the one thought to be its mate, *The Forge of Vulcan*. The art of the Eternal City—its recent paintings as well as its antiquities—strongly influenced Velázquez's frieze of men in this canvas. They eloquently manifest his ability to combine figure studies from ancient sculpture with his contemporaries' skill at expressing emotion, and his own distinctive vision and depth of feeling. He also visited other cities in Italy and found the Venetian artists inspiring. Their quick and open brushwork began making its way into his style of painting as he executed this canvas.

Jacob Receiving Joseph's Blood-Stained Coat
DIEGO VELÁZQUEZ, Spanish, 1599–1660
Monastery of San Lorenzo de El Escorial, Spain. Oil on canvas, 87 3/4 × 98 3/8 in.

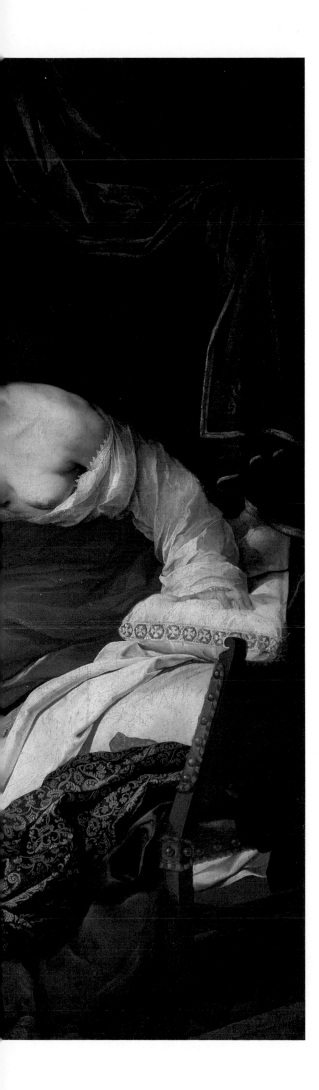

Potiphar, captain of the Pharaoh's guard, purchased Joseph from the Ishmaelites. The Egyptian was impresssed with the Hebrew youth and eventually placed him in charge of his entire household. "Now Joseph was handsome and good-looking," the Bible states, and Potiphar's wife tried to seduce him. Not wanting to betray her husband's trust, Joseph told the woman that he could not perform "this great wickedness, and sin against God." Although he tried to avoid her thereafter, she continued to pursue him. Finally, on a day when all the other men of the household were gone, "she caught him by his garment, saying, 'Lie with me.'" Joseph fled from her presence and from the house, without even bothering to retrieve his robe from her hand. When her husband came home, the spurned woman told him that Joseph "came in to me to insult me," but she had frightened him off by screaming. Enraged, Potiphar had the youth imprisoned (Genesis 39:6–20).

The great Spanish painter of Bible subjects, Bartolomé Esteban Murillo, portrayed a Joseph frozen in indecision in his painting *Joseph and Potiphar's Wife*. While the young man's feet are set to flee the woman's bedroom, his eyes linger on her breasts and the expression on his face speaks of desires not discussed in the Bible story. Despite his momentary indecision, his master's wife already knows that her attempted seduction has failed. The right side of the composition is teeming with the textures of rich textiles, tossed in disarray to represent the passionate desires of Potiphar's wife. By contrast, the rug on which Joseph stands and his fine raiment are tidy.

The tonality of this work is dramatic. The two figures are sharply lighted, and the same illumination brings into view objects that suggest the private chambers of a wealthy couple. Everything else is shrouded in darkness. Even the hand of Potiphar's wife is obscured by shadow as it grabs Joseph's robe. Murillo's use of light and dark translates in moral terms into the struggle between good and evil. In this painting, it is the former that triumphs. Although Joseph landed in jail for resisting the temptations that Potiphar's wife threw his way, he became the steward of the prison. Just as he had previously been Potiphar's slave and became manager of his household, he seemed to turn every situation into an opportunity. As the Bible said, "whatever he did, the Lord made it prosper" (Genesis 39:23).

Joseph and Potiphar's Wife
BARTOLOMÉ ESTEBAN MURILLO, Spanish, 1617–1682
Staatliche Kunstsammlungen Kassel, Germany, Gemäldegalerie Alte Meister. Oil on canvas, 76 5/8 x 95 5/8 in.

Joseph Receiving Pharaoh's Ring

While in prison for alleged infidelities with Potiphar's wife, Joseph interpreted the dream of a fellow inmate, Pharaoh's chief butler. Subsequently returned to the Egyptian monarch's service, the butler remembered Joseph two years later when his master began to experience dreams that none of his wise men could explain. At the servent's recommendation, Pharaoh sent for Joseph, who interpreted his dreams to mean that Egypt would endure seven years of plenty and seven years of want. Pharaoh took heed of the young man's counsel and prepared his nation for a long famine, placing Joseph in charge of his palace and his people. The symbol of Joseph's sudden change of fortune was the gift of Pharaoh's signet ring, which the monarch took from his own hand and put on the young Hebrew's finger (Genesis 41:42). It is this significant moment that the Venetian painter, Giovanni Battista Tiepolo, depicts in *Joseph Receiving Pharaoh's Ring*.

Venice, the greatest trading port in Europe during the 18th century, was full of exotic people. Tiepolo frequently painted turbaned men from the East, and indeed used one of them as a model for Pharaoh in this splendid painting. The Nubian slave at his elbow, seen in silhouette, is another exotic figure, one familiar to Venetians, but alluringly strange to other Europeans.

Two servants who watch the interaction between the handsome protagonists seem somewhat amazed at Pharaoh's beneficence to an outsider. Joseph's seriousness and sincerity are evident in the delicate features attributed to him by the artist, while his strength of character is symbolized by the fluted column behind him. Adding a brassy celebratory note to an otherwise quiet painting are the banners and trumpets in the upper right. They are silhouetted against a pale blue sky that is clear except for three stripes of pink, which match the color of the lining of Joseph's cloak.

Joseph Receiving Pharoah's Ring
GIOVANNI BATTISTA TIEPOLO, Italian, 1696–1770
Dulwich Picture Gallery, London. Oil on canvas,
41 3/4 x 70 3/4 in.

Joseph correctly interpreted Pharaoh's dreams, and thus, after a seven-year period of growth, Egypt and the surrounding region experienced a severe and prolonged famine. Thanks to the monarch's foresight and Joseph's wise counsel, the Egyptian people were prepared, but Canaan, Joseph's homeland, was not so fortunate. In desperation, Jacob sent Joseph's brothers to Egypt to buy corn. And there they encountered their brother, who was then governor of the land. They did not recognize him in his fine robes, however, though he immediately knew them. But he bore them no malice for as he told them much later when he revealed himself to them, "it was not you who sent me here, but God." He filled their sacks with corn, joined them in a tearful reunion, and then asked them to bring their father to Egypt so the family could live out the remaining five years of the famine in security (Genesis 45:4 and 8).

Joseph Recognized by His Brothers by Francois-Pascal-Simon Gérard is a small oil sketch for a larger, more finished canvas. Being a preparatory work, it captures a degree of spontaneity that is unusual in French academic painting. In it, Gérard dresses Joseph in a white robe with a brilliant gold stripe along its border. The same gold is repeated in the costume of the brother in the white turban who kneels to the left of Joseph. The figure in the left foreground is removing his hat, while the one to the far right moves his hand to his forehead in a salaam. Benjamin, the 12th and youngest son of Jacob, and Joseph's full brother, is shown drying his tears.

Painted in the year that saw the outbreak of the French Revolution, *Joseph Recognized by His Brothers* earned second prize in the prestigious Prix de Rome competition. It was an age in which artists searched biblical and classical history to find metaphors for the trauma France was experiencing. The subject of Joseph forgiving his brothers must have had significant political overtones in a nation reeling from class warfare.

As a fashionable portrait painter, Gérard managed to survive the ensuing changes in government during the Terror and later found favor with both Napoleon and the restored monarchy that succeeded him. When he became court painter to King Louis XVIII, he was given the title of baron.

Joseph Recognized by His Brothers
BARON FRANÇOIS-PASCAL-SIMON GÉRARD, French, 1770–1837
Richard L. Feigen & Co., New York. Oil on canvas, 15 x 18 1/8 in.

Joseph in Egypt

JACOPO DA PONTORMO, Italian, 1494–1557

The National Gallery, London. Oil on canvas, 36 ³/₄ x 43 ¹/₈ in

The Saga of Joseph

On his deathbed, Joseph, who was 110 years old, told his brothers "God will visit you, and bring you out of this land to the land which he swore to Abraham, to Isaac, and to Jacob" (Genesis 50:24), thus effectively foreshadowing the central action of the second book of the Old Testament, Exodus, which began immediately after the account of his death.

The saga of Joseph's life remains a mainstay of Judeo-Christian theology. Every generation learns of his dreams, his rise to power, and his reconciliation with his brothers, and draws age-old moral lessons from these stories. In the case of *The Story of Joseph,* which Biagio di Antonio painted in Florence, during the flowering of the Renaissance, the highlights of the patriarch's career were used to help a pair of newlyweds begin their married life together.

Two matching painted wood panels remain from this work, the one illustrated in this volume, which shows episodes from Joseph's early life, and the other, which recalls his career in Egypt. Both panels come from a cassone, or linen chest, one forming the front, the other, the lid. Such chests were commissioned of artists for the maidens of rich families. They were filled—like hope chests—with an array of objects and garments that served as part of a bride's trousseau, and they were decorated with paintings drawn from the tales and moral lessons of ancient history.

Because *cassone* were usually 5 or 6 feet long, but only between 2 or 3 feet tall and deep, the painted panels were rectangular in shape, a size that particularly lent

itself—somewhat like a comic strip—to the telling of a tale in serial fashion. Biagio di Antonio begins his narration with Jacob asking young Joseph to check on his brothers and their flocks. Jacob sits like a prelate in an open, arched loggia with a shallow dome, much like one Brunelleschi, the greatest architect in Florence, might have designed. Next Joseph walks off into the countryside, where he can be seen checking on his siblings through the open arch above Jacob's throne-like chair. In the left background of the panel, he is dumped into a well by his jealous brothers, and in the interior scene in the middle of the painting, the hard-hearted lads present Joseph's bloody coat to their bereaved father. The enslaved Joseph's departure for Egypt is seen on the right. Since the painting's background is a uniform warm tan, broken by mounds of deep green grass, the artist keeps Joseph in the same color tunic in each narrative sequence so that his trail can be easily followed.

A generation after Biagio's activity in Florence, Jacopo da Pontormo was commissioned to paint two *cassone* fronts and a wall decoration for a wealthy Florentine, Pierfrancesco Borgherini. His subject was *Joseph in Egypt.* The artist was only 21 years of age, but his youthful talent had already drawn praise from no less an artist than Michelangelo. Like Biagio before him, he combined a number of incidents in one composition. On the left, Joseph presents his father to Pharaoh, he receives supplicants seeking bread in the center, and on the right he reads a petition as naked youths pull his triumphal carriage through the city. In an upper bedroom of a round building, accessible only by a strange curved stairway, Joseph's father, Jacob, is dying in the presence of his family.

Though Biagio and Pontormo both dealt with a series of scenes in a single setting, the moods of their paintings differ drastically. Biagio allows the viewer's eye to move leisurely from scene to scene in an ordered way, and he highlights the

protagonist throughout. Pontormo, by contrast, mystifies the viewer with his use of irrational variances in the sizes of his figures and the inclusion of people irrelevant to the biblical text, such as those conspicuously walking up the curved staircase. Just as the putti atop the column on the far right imitate sculpture, so the figures ascending the stairs seem to mimic tourists amazed at the wonders of Egypt.

The Renaissance of Biagio's era stressed order, balance, and rationality. These qualities are inherent in the architectural structure that is the setting of two of his episodes and the frame of a third. It is structurally sound, symmetrical, and scaled to human inhabitants. Pontormo's architecture did not—and could not—exist in reality. It is irrational, off balance, and uneasy. A great deal is left unexplained in his painting, such as the meaning of the two nude sculptures that so dominate the horizon. The artist was one of the first of his age to challenge the notion that through idealism one could answer any question and solve any problem. Rather his odd inventions of style express a pessimistic outlook. His art was in the vanguard of an ante-Renaissance movement called Mannerism, which became the dominant style in many areas of Italy and in much of the rest of Europe during the last three quarters of the 16th century. It particularly flourished under royal patronage.

MERCATATI
GVSEPPO
RVBEN
GVSEPPO
GVSEPPO
GVSEPPO
GIACOB
BENIAMI
BENIAMI
GIACOB

The Story of Joseph
BIAGIO DI ANTONIO, Italian, active 1476–1504
The J. Paul Getty Museum, Malibu, California. Tempera on wood panel, 26 1/4 x 58 3/4 in.

MERCATAN

Jacob's Blessing

In his later years, Jacob resided in Egypt with Joseph and his family. Although he was nearly blind, he remained the gallant and benevolent farmer-patriarch, who doted on his youngest son. As the old man neared death, Joseph brought his own two sons, Manasseh and Ephraim, to their grandfather. In a scene reminiscent of that between Jacob and the dying Isaac, the old man blessed Ephraim, the younger of the two, with his right hand, while Joseph tried to guide the appendage, typically reserved for the heir, to the head of the elder grandson, Manasseh. Showing signs of his old vigor, Jacob would not comply, arguing that both of the boys would be great, but that the younger would be the greater. "His descendants shall become a multitude of nations," he prophesied (Genesis 48:19).

Rembrandt captures this family gathering in *Jacob's Blessing*. Even Joseph's wife, Arenath, who seldom makes an appearance in art, is shown, adding a touch of feminine beauty and maternal pride to this study of the three ages of man. Joseph, after his great successes in Egypt, still appears to be the favored son, as his father leans close to tell him about the future of his children. A fur upon the old patriarch's back is a reminder of how as a child he was blessed as the firstborn—through deception—and thereby won the inheritance of his brother Esau.

Rembrandt knew his Bible well and sought friendships in the Jewish quarter of Amsterdam so that he would always have a supply of willing models to bring authenticity to his biblical paintings. While he tells the story of Jacob's blessing accurately and with great sympathy, he is primarily interested in the message behind the tale—that God intended his people to be together as a single family. The men and boys lean toward one another in intimacy and love, forming an equilateral triangle of great strength, and the rich red bed covering links them to Arenath. There are no auxiliary details. Everything in this painting works to foster the telling of the story and to convey the humanity of these personages.

Rembrandt was 47 years of age when he painted this scene, but he was already old beyond his years. He had lost three sons and a beloved wife, and in the very year that he painted this biblical family he lost his home and art collection through bankruptcy. Ironically, during this period of deep personal misfortune, he reached his zenith as a draftsman. One can see this profound skill in the hand and arm of Jacob and in the individualized treatment of all the faces. Even in a reproduction, one can appreciate the sweep of Rembrandt's brushstrokes, emerging from paint boldly laid on the surface of the canvas. Thus, the force of his own personality emerges in this painting along with those of the five individuals he depicted.

Jacob's Blessing
REMBRANDT VAN RIJN, Dutch, 1606–1669
Staatlichen Kunstsammlungen Kassel, Germany, Gemäldegalerie Alte Meister. Oil on canvas, 68 1/2 x 82 1/16 in.

FOLLOWING PAGES

VAN LEYDEN: *The Worship of the Golden Calf* (detail)

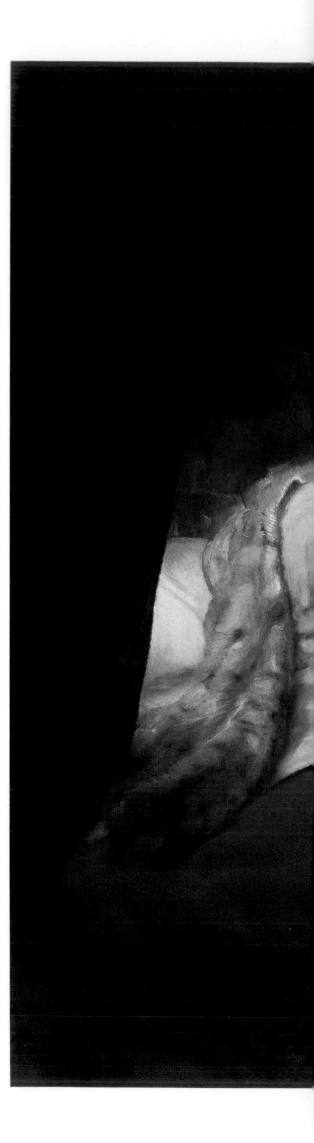

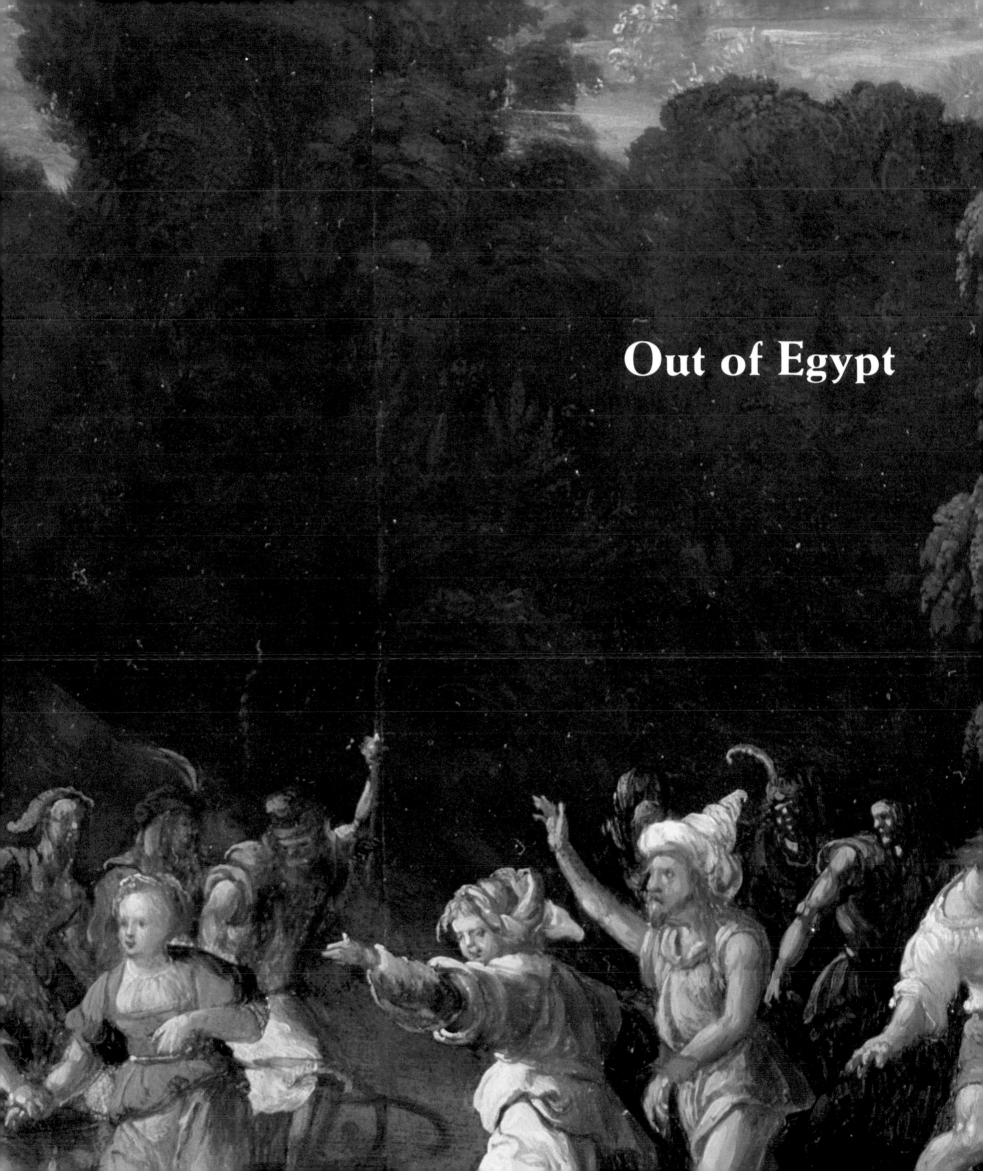

Out of Egypt

The Finding of Moses

The finding of the baby Moses in the shallows of the River Nile occurred centuries after Joseph's service to Pharaoh. The exact number of years separating the lives of the two Hebrew leaders is difficult to determine with accuracy. Some biblical archaeologists believe that Apepi II, a Hyksos, or Semitic, shepherd-king of Egypt, was the Pharaoh who received Joseph, and that Hatshepsut was the Queen of Egypt who raised Moses. Approximately 200 years separated these two rulers. Others think that the daughter of Ramses II brought up Moses, adding an additional 200 years to the chronology. Whichever theory is correct, no one in Moses' day could remember Joseph or any of his children.

The years between Joseph's death and Moses' coming of age were not kind to the Jews of Egypt. As their number and power increased, they became a threat to the indigenous Egyptian population. Even after they were enslaved, they continued to multiply. Finally, Pharaoh determined to exterminate them by putting to death every newborn son of Israel. Among the imperiled was a boy from the house of Levi, the clan of priests. His mother had hidden him until he was three months old; when she couldn't conceal his existence any longer, she made a basket of papyrus (bulrushes) and covered it with tar and pitch so that it was watertight. She then laid the baby in it and set it afloat in the shallows of the Nile, stationing her daughter Miriam nearby to keep an eye on it. Before long, Pharaoh's daughter came to bathe in the river with her retinue of young women. One of the ladies in waiting found the basket and the crying baby. The princess knew immediately that it was one of the Hebrew children, but she adopted him as her own son and named him Moses.

Sometime in the early 1570s, the Venetian painter Paolo Veronese sought a respite from the production of enormous and resplendent palace murals, for which he was famous, by painting this relatively small (for him) canvas. At about the same time, he created a version of the Last Supper, for which he added too many irrelevant figures to suit the Inquisition. Although he argued that his large canvas could hold many figures, he quickly sought to protect himself by changing the name of the work to *The Feast in the House of Levi* (this banquet scene demanded more people than did Jesus' Passover repast with his disciples). In the present work, however, size gives Veronese no license. The addition of male figures to the princess' female retinue simply reflects his familiarity with the noble houses of Venice, in which African slaves were commonplace and dwarfs a treasured rarity.

The two women in the left background are so far away from the foreground action that they might not be part of the narrative at all. The furthest of the two, however, might represent Miriam, Moses' natural sister. If so, she will soon run forward and offer to find the princess a nursemaid for the baby, but at the moment the women of the court are being efficient and admiring mothers. The elongated, blond grace of Pharaoh's daughter is echoed in the slender tree that rises over half the height of the painting above the figure of the baby. Both typically express Veronese's sense of beauty, a vision that he retained during his long and successful career.

The Finding of Moses

PAOLO VERONESE, Italian, 1528–1588

Andrew W. Mellon Collection, National Gallery of Art, Washington, D.C. Oil on canvas, 22 3/4 x 17 1/2 in.

Moses Being Tested by the Pharoah
GIORGIONE, Italian, ca. 1478–1510
Galleria degli Uffizi, Florence. Oil on wood panel, 35 x 28 in.

The Trial of Moses

When Moses discovered that he had been chosen by God to lead the children of Israel out of bondage, he considered himself unfit for the task, saying "I am slow of speech and of tongue" (Exodus 4:10). Ultimately, he remedied his deficiency by making his brother, Aaron, his spokesman.

A legend, separate from the biblical text, explains the origins of his speech impediment. According to the story, Pharaoh was advised to kill him when he was three years old. To decide the boy's fate, the monarch submitted him to a trial by fire. Giorgione, the great Venetian artist of the Renaissance, shows what happened in *Moses Being Tested by the Pharoah*.

Two dishes were presented to the child. One was filled with rubies, the other with burning coals. If little Moses took a ruby, he would be killed. Instead, he took a coal, tried to eat it, and permanently injured his tongue. In Giorgione's version of the story, Pharaoh's daughter, who holds the child, assumes a leading role. Indeed, her father seems to trust her more than his white-bearded advisor. Perhaps Giorgione is suggesting that this dangerous test was her idea, since it gave Moses, her adopted son, a 50–50 chance of survival. At any rate, he did survive. By taking a coal, and thereby "proving" that he was not a threat to the wealth and bounty of Pharoah, he continued to be raised as a prince in the royal household.

In this, the earliest of only 20 extant paintings by Giorgione, the landscape fills two-thirds of the painting and creates a mood of rugged but tamed beauty. The figures, by contrast, are unnaturally formal. The grace with which Giorgione would later imbue the human form—and for which so much of his high reputation rests—had not yet come to him.

Small pictures like this one were known as "cabinet" paintings because they were created for display in small rooms reserved for private delectation. In an age when most paintings were created for public show, Giorgione was one of the earliest artists to specialize in cabinet pictures. Subject matter and certain details were probably dictated by the collectors for whom these works were produced.

The Burning Bush

The life of Moses changed in one day as he went from being a shepherd of his father-in-law's flocks to the leader of the Hebrews. But then much had happened to him already since his childhood in the royal household of Egypt: he had killed an Egyptian who was beating a Hebrew slave, for which he was condemned to death by Pharaoh; he had fled Egypt and gone to live in the land of Midian, where he saved a priest's flock of sheep from a group of raiders; and he married one of the priest's daughters, Zipporah, and had a child with her. He probably thought that he would never see his own people again, but one day when he was on the west side of the great wilderness that separates Egypt from the homeland of the Israelites, specifically on the slopes of Mount Horeb, better known as Sinai, "the angel of the Lord appeared to him in a flame of fire out of the midst of a bush." Attracted to the sight, Moses was surprised to discover that the shrub was not consumed by the flames. Then God spoke to him: "I have seen the affliction of my people who are in Egypt," the Lord said, "And I have come down to deliver them out of the hand of the Egyptians." Then he instructed Moses to go to Pharaoh "that you may bring forth my people, the sons of Israel, out of Egypt" (Exodus 3:7–11). Despite Moses' reluctance to assume so monumental a task, the Lord convinced him to take up his staff—which God imbued with magical powers—and lead his people to freedom.

The relatively unknown Italian artist Jacopo Vignali portrays this critical encounter in *Moses at the Burning Bush*. The shepherd has just heard his name being called from out of the blaze. "Do not come near," it commands. "Put off your shoes from your feet, for the place on which you are standing is holy ground." Moses is stunned but does as he is told, for the voice identifies himself as "the God of your father, the God of Abraham, the God of Isaac, and the God of Jacob" (Exodus 3:6).

Vignali fills the entire height of his canvas with the seated figure of Moses, who is dressed in stylish 17th-century Italian clothing. It was easy for Vignali's contemporaries to identify closely with this man, and to sympathize with him for the awesome responsibility that he is about to assume. One of the sheep in the lower right corner of the canvas looks out at the viewer, but the animal is more than a mere reflection of Moses' occupation; he represents the Israelites, the human flock who will become Moses' charges for the rest of his life. On the ground is the rod that he uses to control his animals. Now it will become an instrument for performing miracles in the cause of his people.

There is a stillness in this painting that suggests quiet reflection. Indeed, its purpose is clearly to inspire viewers to follow the will of God. The only suggestion of movement lies in the brilliant fabric that cascades in nervous folds from Moses' back. Its strong color leads the viewer's straying eye from the myriad details of the painting back to the face of Moses.

Moses at the Burning Bush
JACOPO VIGNALI, Italian, 1592–1664
Bob Jones University Collection of Religious Art, Greenville, South Carolina. Oil on canvas, 39 x 48 3/4 in.

Moses went to Pharaoh as the Lord commanded, but the resolute monarch would not let the Israelites return to their ancestral home. To change his mind, God instructed Moses to devastate the country with ten plagues. After each calamity, Pharaoh agreed to free the Israelites, but each time he changed his mind. Among the afflictions that beset Egypt were the turning of the country's rivers to blood; infestations of frogs, lice, and flies; an outbreak of boils; a horrific hailstorm; vast swarms of locusts; a period of unremitting darkness; and the slaying of the firstborn males.

The seventh plague, a destructive storm of hail, rain, and fire, was the subject of a painting by Joseph Mallord William Turner, one that he incorrectly titled *The Fifth Plague of Egypt* (the Bible itself orders the plagues differently in different places). The last plague, the death of the Egyptians'

firstborn sons and animals, was depicted by Erastus Salisbury Field in the *The Burial of the Firstborn of Egypt.*

The cataclysmic aspect of hail, rain, and fire would certainly have appealed to Turner's romantic nature, and he was inspired to make of this disaster a grandly dramatic landscape, the first of many to come. The biblical description gave him plenty to envision, saying "there was hail, and fire flashing continually in the midst of the hail" and that it "struck down everything that was in the field throughout all the land of Egypt, both man and beast; and . . . every plant . . . and shattered every tree" (Exodus 9:24–25). Turner captures all of these elements, but he also adds original touches of great power and majesty: the burnished brown and gold clouds that swirl into a great vortex, the brilliantly lighted white pyramid and city in the center of the composition, and the dead horse and people in the foreground. His use of two black triangular wedges that extend into the canvas from either side and divide the composition into quarters is a radical concept. Their dark tonalities give an added sense of glow to the colors above and below them. This essay in motion, luminosity, atmosphere, and dramatic subject matter led to others in which Turner used the same elements. Soon they were his specialty, and he became famous for landscapes that were more daring and grander than any that had been painted before.

Erastus Salisbury Field, who lived in a village in the hills of western Massachusetts, painted the ten plagues of Egypt for the walls of his local church. He was drawn to the spiritual lessons inherent in these magical episodes, but he also saw in the story of Israel's deliverance out of Egypt a persuasive argument for the end of slavery in America. *The Burial of the Firstborn of Egypt*, to Field's way of thinking, emphasized the lengths to which God was prepared to go in his desire to punish

Burial of the Firstborn of Egypt
ERASTUS SALISBURY FIELD, American, 1805–1900
Museum of Fine Arts, Springfield, Massachusetts. Oil on
canvas, 33 ¹/₄ x 39 ¹/₄ in.

DETAIL
The Fifth Plague of Egypt
J.M. W. TURNER

>

DETAIL

slaveholders. Living in a region that had never known a slave economy, and one that was virtually untouched by the Civil War, Field probably encountered a fair amount of apathy among his hardworking neighbors when it came to the subject of abolition and its aftermath. Nevertheless, it was a topic of deep concern to him, one to which he devoted almost all of his aesthetic efforts in the decade following the Civil War.

Both Turner and Field wanted to make grand statements with their paintings of the plagues of Egypt, and they succeeded, but with entirely different visual means. Turner, well schooled in art, knew the neoclassical paintings of Claude Lorrain and Nicolas Poussin, and he studied their efforts to introduce into landscape painting dramatic effects through the use of light and atmosphere. In *The Fifth Plague of Egypt*, he magnified and exaggerated these elements in order to dwarf the land and to make the storm itself the primary subject. Field, by contrast, was primarily self-taught, except for a brief period spent in the New York studio of Samuel F. B. Morse. When not limning portraits of family members and neighbors, he depended for visual ideas on black-and-white book illustrations such as those of the English artist John Martin. Like Turner, Field exaggerated what he saw, turning visual elements into patterns. In *The Burial of the Firstborn of Egypt* he elongates the avenue to allow a seemingly endless repetition of columns. The motif of a white pall carried by more people than could ordinarily crowd around a casket is also repeated, setting up an incessant rhythm that makes its point like the drumming of taps.

The Fifth Plague of Egypt

JOSEPH MALLORD WILLIAM TURNER,
English, 1775–1851

Gift in memory of Evan F. Lilly, Indianapolis Museum of Art. Oil on canvas, 48 × 72 in.

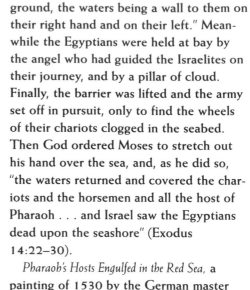

The annihilation of the firstborn sons of Egypt forced Pharaoh to free the Israelites. After 430 years, they could finally return to the "land flowing with milk and honey" (Exodus 13:5). But they had no sooner begun their trek across the wilderness, then Pharaoh had second thoughts about their release, and set out to enslave them once more, taking with him a large army, including 600 chariots. The Egyptians caught up to Moses and his followers at the banks of the Red Sea. With the sea before them and Pharaoh's host behind them, the Israelites were trapped. But that night a great east wind arose to part the waters, and the following morning they

"went into the midst of the sea on dry ground, the waters being a wall to them on their right hand and on their left." Meanwhile the Egyptians were held at bay by the angel who had guided the Israelites on their journey, and by a pillar of cloud. Finally, the barrier was lifted and the army set off in pursuit, only to find the wheels of their chariots clogged in the seabed. Then God ordered Moses to stretch out his hand over the sea, and, as he did so, "the waters returned and covered the chariots and the horsemen and all the host of Pharaoh . . . and Israel saw the Egyptians dead upon the seashore" (Exodus 14:22–30).

Pharaoh's Hosts Engulfed in the Red Sea, a painting of 1530 by the German master Lucas Cranach the Elder, creates a striking visual simile between the wall of water and a mountain. The shapes of the standing waves resemble craggy peaks, especially those in the Chinese paintings of Cranach's day, and the mountain above the Israelites is like a great wave. Aside from this almost poetic interpretation of the biblical story, Cranach's work is quite literal and didactic, drawing its inspiration from old Judgment Day paintings with their diverse groups of the Saved and the Damned. With its teaming masses of heads and bodies representing Pharaoh's armies and Moses' followers, this painting is more impressive in its compositional whole than in its individual details.

Benjamin West's unfinished painting of 1792, *Pharaoh and His Host Lost in the Red Sea,* shows Moses in the upper left, stretching out his arm to return the waters to their ordinary flow. Below him is a terrified Egyptian warrior whose chariot, represented by a single wheel in the lower left, sinks into the seabed. The Israelites' guardian angel is at the top of the picture, arched over a group of women and their frightened children. Below them one can see the outlines of a horse's head and neck, along with other roughly sketched forms in the lower right corner of the canvas. The dry path between the walls of water is not indicated. One can not determine from the present state of the painting what the finished work would have looked like.

West's sketchy canvas is selective and

Pharaoh and His Host Lost in the Red Sea

BENJAMIN WEST, American, 1738–1820

Worcester Art Museum, Massachusetts. Oil on canvas, 38 1/4 × 30 in.

suggestive; Cranach's is very inclusive and literal. By opposite means, each artist comments on the biblical story, telling far more than meets the eye. In West's patterns of dark diagonals and lighter spirals and arcs, and in his confused tangle of figures, he manages to suggest the enormous power of God. By contrast, the visual simplicity of Cranach's work focuses the viewer on the more human dimensions of the story, the large mass of those fleeing compared to that of the pursuing army, and the vast terrain that encompassed the Israelites' journey.

Lucas Cranach the Elder was a close friend and neighbor of Martin Luther and knew the Bible primarily through the Reformer's sermons. In fact, he was called "the painter to the Reformation." In *Pharaoh's Hosts,* he clearly offers his audience a message of hope, suggesting that, as God saved the Israelites and destroyed their enemies, so too would he prevail against the Roman Catholics on behalf of the new Protestants. Moses, in this instance, does not represent God, but a good and kindly prince, like one of the three successive Electors of Saxony—loyal Lutherans all—whom Cranach served.

West became president of the Royal Academy at about the time that he was working on his painting of *Pharaoh and His Host Lost in the Red Sea.* In its various states of completion, one can readily see the

Pharaoh's Hosts Engulfed in the Red Sea
LUCAS CRANACH THE ELDER, German, 1472–1553
Alte Pinakothek, Munich. Oil on wood panel, 32 1/4 x 46 in.

methodology of the artist. He began the composition by sketching it on the canvas. He next scrubbed in the areas of deeper shadow with dark earth tones, and, finally, he began to model the figures in color before abandoning the composition. Today the painting is valued and exhibited along with finished works because it shows the hand of an inspired and spirited talent working out ideas, just as Cranach's work is valued as a charming expression of dogma.

The Gathering of Manna

BACCHIACCA, Italian, 1494–1557

Samuel H. Kress Collection, National Gallery of Art, Washington, D.C. Oil on wood panel, 44 x 37 ¹/₂ in.

Manna from Heaven

Following their departure from Egypt, the Israelites wandered in the wilderness for 40 years. After two and a half months, they found themselves short of food and exceptionally cranky. God heard their complaints, however, and created a heavenly solution to their hunger problem: Every morning he sent manna from heaven, "fine as hoarfrost on the ground." It was white, shaped like coriander seed, "and the taste of it was like wafers made of honey." Moses told his followers to collect enough of the heavenly bread every morning to nourish the entire tribe, and on the sixth day to collect for the Sabbath as well, since on that day gathering food, like all other labors, was taboo. They were also commanded to keep a sample of God's gift for all time, so a jar of it went into the ark of the covenant. During the duration of the Jews' sojourn in the wilderness, this unique foodstuff sustained them (Exodus 16:14-35).

In his charming work *The Gathering of Manna*, the mid-16th century Italian artist known as Bacchiacca depicts Moses instructing his people to collect stores of the bread-like food for the Sabbath. About 100 years later, the French artist Nicolas Poussin emphasized the miraculous and sacramental aspects of the event in his *Manna from Heaven*.

According to the biblical account, the Israelites "despoiled the Egyptians" of gold and silver jewelry and clothing before heading into the desert. They also took herds and flocks of cattle with them (Exodus 12:35–38). How Bacchiacca got the idea that there were also giraffes and civet cats may never be known, but he does create a rich and exotic gathering! He organizes this menagerie, along with his human characters, in a loose spiral around the tree in the middle of the composition, and unifies them through a soft overall tonality that ranges from the blue of the sky and background landscape to the pink of Moses' robe. Bright red brings the viewer's eye to the woman who pours her collection of manna into a great brass vessel in preparation for the designated day of rest.

A Florentine who maintained the noble style of the High Renaissance well after its greatest practitioners were dead, Bacchiacca painted many scenes from the Old Testament. Because he makes Moses the center of his composition—while Poussin relegates him, with Aaron, to the middle distance—the meaning of his painting might be found in this pivotal figure. Since he is pointing with his staff at the woman storing manna for the Sabbath, perhaps Bacchiacca is exhorting his viewers to keep Moses' laws. For the affluent citizens of Florence, tempted perhaps to become complacent in their wealth, this may simply have been a lesson about storing the riches of today for the needs of tomorrow.

Poussin focuses on the very first encounter of the Jews with their heavenly food, and in so doing concerns himself primarily with its saving grace. So desperately hungry have the wanderers become, in Poussin's view, that one woman in the lower left corner of the canvas has had to remove her child from her breast and offer her milk to the famished old woman in the yellow-orange gown, probably her mother. The nurturing woman has appeared as a

theme in art since the Middle Ages, when images showed the Virgin Mary offering her breast as succor to the masses in need of spiritual food. The man in the red toga who watches is the one who grouses, "Would that we had died by the hand of the Lord in the land of Egypt, when we sat by the fleshpots and ate bread to the full" (Exodus 16:3). He has not noticed yet that a miracle is taking place just steps away from him.

In a letter to one of his friends, Poussin discussed the literary and psychological content of his *Manna from Heaven*, so art historians are well aware of his intent. For him the rain of manna offered a striking counterpart to the Sacrament of Holy Communion, in which the body of Jesus is remembered through the ingestion of unleavened wafers called the Bread of Life. A major series illustrating the Seven Sacraments of the Roman Catholic Church occupied the great artist from 1636 to 1640.

FOLLOWING PAGES

DETAIL
Manna from Heaven

Manna from Heaven
NICOLAS POUSSIN, French, 1594–1665
Musée du Louvre, Paris. Oil on canvas, 57 1/8 × 78 in.

Not long after manna was given to them to feed their hunger, the people of Israel were without water and complained bitterly. "So Moses cried to the Lord, 'What shall I do with this people? They are almost ready to stone me'" (Exodus 17:4). In reply, God instructed Moses to take some of the Hebrew elders with him to a specified rock, strike it with the rod that he had used to part the Red Sea, and water would spring forth.

In *Moses Striking the Rock*, the early 17th-century Dutch master Joachim Antoniszoon Wtewael presents a brilliant celebration of this miracle. Arranged in a sweeping, S-shaped curve are some 40 or more people and about half as many animals, all enjoying the waters of life that spout from the rocky promontory in three clear, arching streams. The woman who encloses the composition in the lower left corner of the painting is posed like an ancient Roman sculpture. Though in shadow, she seems to be satisfied with the miracle Moses has wrought. Lining the bottom of the picture, amid the finely painted animals, is a highly realistic and unusual still life composition of pots, jugs, and baskets. The soft pastel colors of the scene bleach into grays beyond the trees where more Israelites are arriving to quench their thirst. Aaron, standing next to his brother Moses, almost leaps in delight at yet another deliverance from disaster.

A few years before Wtewael created his stirring composition, the great Flemish painter Jacob Jordaens turned to the same subject. His composition is also crowded with people and animals, but he adopts a closer vantage point than his predecessor. He doesn't even show the rock or the water, for his interest is centered entirely on his characters and their reactions to the miracle. The place that he has created is somewhat eerie, with an almost blinding supernatural light flooding an otherwise dark scene. A mother holds her baby up to witness this theophanic miracle, and others

Moses Striking the Rock

JOACHIM ANTONISZOON WTEWAEL, Dutch,
ca.1566–1638

Ailsa Mellon Bruce Fund, National Gallery of Art,
Washington, D.C. Oil on wood panel, 17 1/2 x 26 1/4 in

shield their eyes to see better. One whose face cannot be seen thrusts a gleaming brass ewer above the others as a symbol of the people's faith in Moses. The father whose strong bare back is toward the viewer tells his son exactly how to aid the patriarch but also how to enhance his view of the action. Jordaens' young and aggressive Moses shouts a prayer to God, while guiding his slim staff to the place where he hopes to find water.

Wtewael was the last of the Mannerist painters in Utrecht, a Roman Catholic stronghold within the Protestant territories of the Netherlands. His elongated figures in balletic poses and his arbitrary divisions of space were typical of Mannerism, a style that had started in Italy in the second quarter of the 16th century. In Wtewael's day the style was rapidly giving way to more naturalistic modes of painting, but his combination of high realism—as seen in the foreground pots and pans—and an old-fashioned way of rendering people had great appeal for the conservatives of his city. His works enabled them to keep in touch with their glorious artistic past and with the symbols of their prosperity.

Antwerp had been another center for Mannerist painting, but the heroic style of Peter Paul Rubens, the city's foremost artist, accelerated its demise. Still, elements of the old style linger in Jordaens' *Moses Striking Water from the Rock,* with its acidic and somewhat lurid colors and its figures piled up three and four deep.

Each of these artists is single-minded in his concentration on just one aspect of the episode. Ironically, Wtewael, whose style of painting called attention to the spiritual aspects of this story, was really interested in the miracle's physical dimensions, whereas Jordaens, who emphasized the physicality of his characters, was focused on the story's spiritual aspects.

Moses Striking Water from the Rock
JACOB JORDAENS, Flemish, 1593–1678
Staatliche Kunsthalle, Karlsruhe, Germany. Oil on wood panel,
81 x 70 in.

The Ten Commandments

Moses Receiving the Tablets of the Law

MARC CHAGALL, Russian, 1887–1985

Musée National Message Biblique Marc Chagall, Nice, France. Oil on canvas, 92 3/4 x 102 15/16 in.

No image from the Hebrew Bible is better known than that of Moses with the two "tables of stone, written with the finger of God" (Exodus 31:18). Nor is there a theophany described in more magnificently simple words: "The glory of the Lord settled on Mount Sinai . . . like a devouring fire on the top of the mountain." And Moses entered the cloud of smoke that enveloped the mountain and was with God for 40 days and 40 nights (Exodus 24:16–18).

The Ten Commandments were the most important outgrowth of Moses' days with God, and images of the lawgiver have had a prominent place in mural decoration since the 3rd century A.D. In the exuberant painting *Moses Receiving the Tablets of the Law*, Marc Chagall chooses a less than literal approach to this event by showing the two stones with only vague marks across their surface. The hand of God is etching laws into one of them even as they are given to Moses, whose mouth is open in joyous praise. Chagall, who was raised in Judaism, knew that the tablets also contained a multitude of other laws. He no doubt has relegated them to the Torah carried by an angel in the area below the tablets. The Israelites along the lower margins of the picture prepare to receive God's edicts with ritual worship.

Chagall insisted that his almost surrealistic image was a direct reflection of how the story of Moses was told to him in his childhood. The fiery glory of God—to him the most compelling aspect of the tale—is represented by golden hues, with smudges of gray indicating smoke. The cloud that hid Moses from his people is not shown, but the lawgiver's robe and the mountain itself are composed of billowing forms. The rabbi in the lower right corner evokes thoughts of the artist's youth in Vitebsk, Russia. He may even be the one who first told Chagall the tale.

Chagall was a prominent artist in Russia immediately after the Revolution. He founded a liberal art academy in his home district, and designed and painted scenery for the Yiddish Theater in Moscow. He also established a solid reputation in Paris, which became his home in the days when modernism was first coming into its own.

In his later years, he designed stained glass windows featuring the 12 tribes of Israel for a hospital in Jerusalem, and painted large murals for the great opera houses of Paris and New York. His highly personal, inimitable vision made him one of the most popular of the giants of 20th-century art. Throughout his unusually successful career, however, he never lost sight of his childhood visions. They, above all else, formed his style.

Unlike Chagall, José de Ribera, a Spaniard who lived most of his life in Naples (then a Spanish possession), was not interested in exploring his own memories. Nor was he interested in Mount Sinai; never in his life did he paint a landscape. Rather, he was intent on creating sympathetic, humanistic "portraits" of the saints and learned men. His *Moses* is a case in point. Pensive in this penultimate moment, the lawgiver appears to be a teacher through and through, instructing his people in the ways of the Lord with patience, but also knowing how difficult it is for them to keep God's commandments. His furry white beard tinged with blond highlights and his high forehead echo the basic form of the tablets in his hands. Rays of light emanate from his brow in the manner that artists often used to convey that "the skin of Moses' face shone" (Exodus 34:35).

Ribera and Chagall shared the same impetus as artists: to create works that would teach and, at the same time, inspire. And, by a strange coincidence, each of their Moses paintings was part a of larger body of work. Ribera's was commissioned in 1638 by a brotherhood of Neopolitan monks as was one of a group of paintings for their church (it still hangs there), whereas Chagall's was created for the Museum of the Biblical Message in Nice, sponsored by the French government to celebrate the artist's religious works.

Moses

JOSÉ DE RIBERA, Spanish, 1591–1652

Chiesa della Certosa di San Martino, Naples. Oil on canvas, 65¹/₂ x 37⁷/₈ in.

The Worship of the Golden Calf

Aaron, Moses' older brother and chief aide, was a sculptor, probably the first practitioner of the art identified as such in recorded history. During Moses' lengthy stay on Mount Sinai, where he communed with God, his "stiff-necked" followers, exasperated by their wanderings in the desert, demanded that Aaron create an idol who could lead them out of their predicament. Reluctantly he agreed to do as they asked and from their golden earrings he "made a molten calf." He probably did so by modeling the animal in clay and then casting it through an ancient technique called *sand casting*. The Israelites were delighted by this shining image and honored it with offerings, but their worship quickly degenerated into a bacchanal.

When God told Moses of his people's behavior, the lawgiver begged the Lord not to punish them for their sins. When he actually saw them dancing around the golden calf, however, he lost his temper. Throwing down the tablets containing the Ten Commandments, he demanded to know "Who is on the Lord's side? Let him come to me." Those who responded were told to slay the others. In the ensuing melee, 3,000 idol worshippers died (Exodus 32:1–29).

In *The Worship of the Golden Calf* by the 16th-century artist Lucas van Leyden, the idol takes second place to the images of eating and dancing. The artist fills the foreground with picnicking gourmands, and the middle ground, with physical fitness enthusiasts. If one looks hard, one can find the tiny figures of Moses and Joshua descending the mountain in the left background under ominous black shadows and gray clouds.

Filippino Lippi, by contrast, makes the bovine statue the principal focus of his painting. Drawing on a knowledge of antiquity that is surprising in its depth even for an Italian artist of the Renaissance, when the study of ancient history had a great revival, he makes his idol not a golden calf but rather the Egyptian god Apis, the sacred bull, identified by the crescent moon on his shoulder. Because the cult of Apis was associated with the River Nile, worship of the idol in Egypt was conspicuous. No doubt the Israelites would have been quite familiar with the god from their years in bondage. Thus, Lippi offers an interesting and even convincing corollary between the Egyptian religion at the time of the Jews' captivity and this biblical story.

During his own lifetime, Lippi's interest in and knowledge of ancient history was well known and his talent as a painter, celebrated. Lorenzo de' Medici, the greatest art patron of the age, referred to him as "superior to Apelles," a reference to the legendary Greek painter of the 4th-century B.C. By contrast, Lucas van Leyden was not the object of praise from his critics, who considered his figures to be rather ploddingly dependent on caricature and anecdote. Today, however, he is recognized as one of the most skilled and prodigious printmakers of all time. Like his etchings, engravings, and woodcuts, his paintings display a deft technique, characterized by brushwork that is sure and quick and an inventive imagination.

The Worship of the Egyptian Bull-God Apis (Golden Calf)
FILIPPINO LIPPI, Italian, 1457(?)–1504
The National Gallery, London. Oil on wood panel, 30 3/4 x 54 in.

DETAIL
FOLLOWING PAGES

The Worship of the Golden Calf
(central panel)
LUCAS VAN LEYDEN, Dutch, 1494–1533
Rijksmuseum, Amsterdam. Oil on wood panel, 36 5/8 x 26 3/8 in.

The Scapegoat
WILLIAM HOLMAN HUNT, English, 1827–1910
City of Manchester Art Galleries, England. Oil on canvas,
13 1/4 x 18 1/16 .in.

The Scapegoat

In the Book of Leviticus, two male goats were specified as "sin offerings" for the Day of Atonement. One was to be sacrificed at the high altar, and the second was to be the scapegoat: he would receive all the iniquities, transgressions, and sins of the people of Israel—through the laying-on of hands by a priest—after which he would be freed in the wilderness to carry "their iniquities . . . to a solitary land" (Leviticus 16:10 and 22).

In the mid-19th century, William Holman Hunt, who was scouting in the Holy Land for biblical subjects, came upon the history of the scapegoat. After consulting the Talmud on the subject, he decided to paint it. He chose the wicked city of Sodom as the backdrop for the work, thereby emphasizing the enormity of the sins the goat had to expiate. Clearly, he was thinking of the animal as a type of redeeming Christ. After much research, the artist discovered that the location of Sodom was thought to have been at the southern end of the Dead Sea, so he set off for that site to paint. To be as accurate as possible, he tried to time his trip so that he would be at the Dead Sea on the Day of Atonement (October 2, 1854), but he did not arrive until later in the month.

A rainbow appeared on the day that Hunt was sketching. Although he saw it above Sodom, the most memorable scene of God's wrath, he associated it with the rainbow that appeared to Noah as a symbol of God's covenant after the flood. He also saw the skeleton of a camel, which he included in the painting, without explanation, at the foot of the rainbow. There is also a wild ibex to the left of the scapegoat. To render this creature, Hunt used the skull of a Sinaitic ibex as a model. The sacrificial goat who has been chosen to die is approaching his mission rather gingerly. The dramatic lighting of yellow and pink over a blue and pink landscape is not invented. The artist saw it by bright moonlight.

Around the goat's head is a red ribbon. This represents a fillet which the priest would have affixed to the animal according to Talmudic instruction. It was meant to symbolize the marks that the priest's bloody fingers would have left on the goat's head during the ceremonial laying-on of hands if he had actually slaughtered the beast. Hunt could not find out how this ribbon was supposed to be attached, "so I merely placed it round about the horns to suggest the crown of thorns," he wrote in his diary on February 14, 1855.

Determined to paint only subjects of moral or social significance, and to base them on direct studies from nature, Hunt produced a number of mawkish paintings. This one, however, became famous in the second half of the 19th century, and even today one must respect it for the artist's fanatical devotion to authenticity.

The Brazen Serpent

To this day, a staff with snakes coiled around it is used as the symbol of a physician. It has its origins in the sacred serpents of Aesculapius, the Greco-Roman god of healing. The bronze serpent made by Moses at the command of God is another, earlier occasion when snakes appeared in a therapeutic context.

The bronze serpent was fashioned toward the end of the Israelite's 40-year sojourn in the wilderness. Once again they were complaining about their unfortunate lifestyle. This time they were particularly vocal about the "worthless food." Angered by their pettiness, which reflected a lack of faith, God sent down "fiery serpents" to punish them, and indeed many Israelites were killed by the deadly reptiles. Rather quickly repentant, the survivors appealed to Moses for help. As usual, he did their bidding, asking God to remove the snakes. In response, the Lord told Moses to fashion a serpent of bronze, set it on a pole, "and every one who is bitten, when he sees it, shall live." And so it was. This totem became an object of worship for the Jews, until, around 700 B.C., when King Hezekiah "broke in pieces the bronze serpent that Moses had made, for until those days the people of Israel had burned incense to it; it was called Nehushtan" (2 Kings 18:4).

Charles Le Brun, the 17th-century author of *The Method of Learning to Draw the Passions*, could have used his painting *The Brazen Serpent* to illustrate his treatise, for among its 21 figures are a wide range of deep emotions. To the left of center is Moses commanding the hysterical Israelites to look at his handiwork. Some gratefully comply, others do so sorrowfully, their arms cradling their dead loved ones. One woman in the lower right corner is in the throes of death. Frozen in agony, she gasps for breath, her eyes rolled back. The youth near her nimbly dodges a corpse as he

spies a serpent. Another tries to pull himself to the safety of the top of one of the huge rocks that constitute the landscape.

Le Brun was not only an artist himself, he was also the manager of the grandest program of royal decoration to take place in the Western world since the ancient Roman emperors. Commanding thousands of artisans, he decorated the two largest royal palaces in Europe, the Louvre and Versailles, filling them with tapestries, chandeliers, mirrors, and furniture, all of which were designed under his supervision. Not a doorknob was made without his approval. He also headed the Academy of Arts and formulated its philosophy and curriculum.

When he was almost 70, he was accused by his detractors of being unable to paint without the help of others. In response, he swiftly executed a huge canvas which so pleased Louis XIV that he painted an entire series of other large works, taking the life of Moses as his theme.

Though rather grandiose, this painting, which relates to Le Brun's late series of works on Moses, inspires awe in its attempt to capture the Israelites' frenzy and rapture as they once more escape trouble of their own making through Moses' intercession with God. Though the New Testament interpreted the fiery serpents as representations of Satan, and the brazen serpent as an evocation of the crucified Christ, the court of Louis XIV focused more on the figure of Moses, who was seen as an example of a good, just, and absolute ruler. Indeed, courtiers flattered their King by comparing him to the Hebrew lawgiver.

The Brazen Serpent
CHARLES LE BRUN, French, 1619–1690
City of Bristol Museum and Art Gallery, England. Oil on canvas, 36 1/16 x 51 1/8 in.

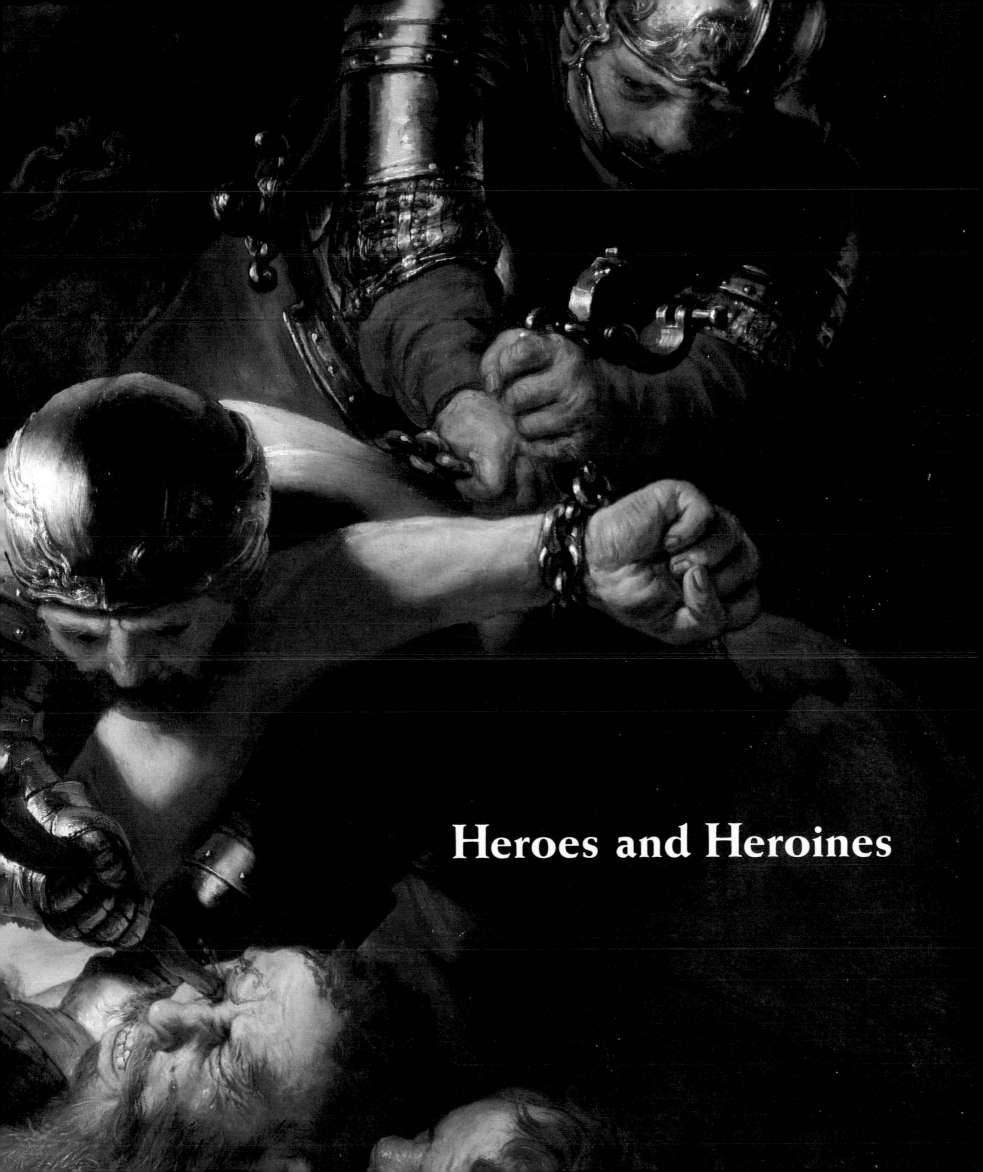

Heroes and Heroines

Balaam and the Ass

In a literature abounding with the angelic manifestations of God, a theophany in the form of an ass is a welcome touch of lightheartedness.

The use of a lowly beast of burden to work God's will occurred as the Israelites were coming to the end of their long sojourn in the desert and nearing sight of the Promised Land. Because they had grown to a sizable force over the years, Balak, the king of Moab, had come to fear them. To assuage his concerns, he sent princes to Mesopotamia to ask the famous diviner, Balaam, to curse the Israelites. At first Balaam refused, but the offer of a huge fee ultimately bought his services. He set out for Moab on his old and trusted donkey, but on the way the animal was stopped three times by the angel of the Lord standing in its path. Only the donkey could see the angel, so each time that it stopped, Balaam beat the poor beast with his staff, until finally God opened the animal's mouth and it said, "What have I done to you, that you have struck me these three times?" This remarkable utterance opened Balaam's eyes and he, too, saw the angel.

The angel's sword was drawn—a detail ignored by Cecco Bravo in *Balaam and the Ass*—as he told the diviner, "Your way is perverse before me" (Numbers 22:28 and 32). Rather than go back to Mesopotamia, which was his first reaction, the diviner was ordered by the angel to serve as an agent of God—or else!—so he continued on to Moab. When he arrived, he *blessed* the Israelites four times before King Balak, instead of *cursing* them as he had been hired to do. The whole event impressed no one, and he was out both his fee and traveling expenses on a journey that, according to biblical scholars, involved a 40-day round trip.

The ass receives bad treatment not only from his master in Cecco Bravo's painting but also from the angel, who tugs on the animal's ear. The heavenly messenger seems more surprised than Balaam at the words coming from the animal's mouth (along with foamy saliva). For Balaam, the discovery of the angel's presence has not yet come.

Cecco Bravo imbues his composition with strong contrasts of light and dark, a sharply lowered viewpoint, and the rich use of the color red, elements that had been reserved by Italian artists since the time of the great Titian for high moments of emotion and drama. But in *Balaam and the Ass* they are unable to lift the scene above the melodramatic or perhaps tragicomic. Though painted by one of the leading artists of 16th-century Florence, this work has the endearing quality of a 19th-century Neopolitan operetta.

Balaam and the Ass
CECCO BRAVO (FRANCESCO MONTELATICI), Italian, 1601–1661
Richard L. Feigen & Co., New York. Oil on canvas, 35 1/16 x 29 1/2 in.

PRECEDING PAGES
REMBRANDT: *The Blinding of Samson* (detail)

Manoah's Sacrifice

CLAES CORNELISZOON MOEYAERT, Dutch, ca.
1592–1655

Richard L. Feigen & Co., New York. Oil on canvas,
39 1/8 x 52 in.

Manoah's Sacrifice

Moses died in the desert, but his people reached their promised destination, the land of Canaan. Though they fought hard to win back their ancient homeland, they were plagued by internal upheaval and political disunity. Even worse, they were surrounded by enemy Philistines. After two centuries of chaos and warfare, a succession of 12 heroes—called judges—rose up from the tribes of Israel to save their people from the oppressors. Among the last of these was Samson.

Samson's father, Manoah, was married to a woman who was barren. But a messenger of God came to her and announced that she would give birth to a son who would "begin to deliver Israel from the hands of the Philistines." The messenger also warned her not to drink wine or liquor or eat anything unclean during her pregnancy and not to cut the child's hair after he was born. When he heard the news, her incredulous husband sought out the messenger and plied him with questions. By way of an

answer, the stranger suggested that Manoah make a sacrifice to the Lord. During the ritual, the messenger appeared once more, this time as an angel in the flame of the altar. Manoah and his wife fell to the ground, the former exclaiming, "We shall surely die, for we have seen God." But his wife assured him that the Lord only meant good things. She dedicated her son to his service and named him Samson (Judges 13:5 and 22).

Like Abraham and Sarah, the parents of Isaac, and Elkanah and Hannah, the parents of Samuel, Manoah and his wife were chosen by God to give birth after long years of childlessness to a hero of Israel. The announcement of this unexpected pregnancy gave the Dutch 17th-century master Claes Corneliszoon Moeyaert an opportunity to show the couple's amazement in *Manoah's Sacrifice*. The news is literally knocking the wife off her feet. A goat lies ready for the ritual in the lower right corner of the canvas, while the dead animal's friend stands nearby, disturbed by the smell of blood and smoke in the air.

Moeyaert's setting is a contemporary village with ruined fortresses. During the artist's lifetime, such structures were becoming increasingly prevalent on the Dutch landscape as the northern provinces of the Netherlands fought against the Spanish-dominated lowlands for their independence. To these Calvinists, Samson was a special hero, for, as they struggled to uphold their principles in the midst of a numerically superior Catholic populace, so Samson stood alone and triumphed against the powerful Philistines. Like the Dutch, he derived his strength from an unswerving adherence to his religious practices. To Moeyaert's contemporaries, the parents of Samson were exemplars of the patriotic citizen, because they were willing to send their son off to fight the enemy.

Delilah

Samson grew to manhood, married, had a child, and won a great victory over the Philistines by slaying 1,000 of their number with the jawbone of an ass. Then he fell in love with a woman who lived in the valley of Sorek, Delilah by name. She became his undoing, for at the behest of the Philistines she discovered the source of his incredible strength—his uncut hair— and sold his secret to his enemies. Though her tale is told in a spare 16 verses of the Bible, she has been remembered through the ages as the epitome of the fascinating and deceitful woman.

Gustave Moreau's painting, now called *Delilah*, was originally displayed under the title *Biblical Courtesan* It perhaps was meant to comment on the highly paid prostitutes of the artist's day who set Paris fashions and enjoyed a public fame similar to that of today's rock stars. In Moreau's vision, Delilah is sensuously enthroned in the Temple of Love, where she plots Samson's downfall in splendid, though vulgar, isolation, her only company being some red doves who have flown in through the recesses of the temple. The flowers strewn at her bare feet and at her elbows imply a number of suitors. Her virginal white costume is theatrical, shameless, and with enough ornamentation to raise the eyebrow of a banker . . . or a chorus girl. The touch of bright red is clue enough to her true nature.

As with Salome, the New Testament femme fatale whose lascivious dancing won her the head of John the Baptist, Delilah caused the downfall of a man pledged from infancy to the service of God. Salome was another of Moreau's favorite subjects, as were Semele and the Sphinx, also destructive seductresses, albeit less successful ones (Semele was destroyed by her lover Zeus; the Sphinx, whom Moreau pictured with a female face and breasts, was outwitted by Oedipus).

Independently wealthy, Moreau did not attempt to sell his work. He developed his bizarre and highly personal style apart from the established art world. Still, he exhibited often and was pursued by the Ecole des Beaux-Arts to teach, which he did during the last three years of his life. He was not an academician, believing instead that an artist should search his inner self for images. Because of his independent nature, he became a hero to a younger generation of artists and numbered Henri Matisse and Georges Rouault among his students. After Moreau's death, Rouault became the first curator of a Paris museum devoted to his teacher's art. It is housed in Moreau's former home.

Delilah
GUSTAVE MOREAU, French, 1826–1898
Museo de Arte de Ponce, Puerto Rico. Oil on canvas, 32 x 26 in.

Samson's Downfall

Although Samson was a womanizer, his Nazarite vows, which bound him to God when he was still in his mother's womb, had never been broken. He did not allow alcohol to pass his lips, he avoided the bodies of the dead, and he never cut his hair. When he fell in love with Delilah, she was immediately commissioned at a high price by the Philistines to learn the secret of his strength. Ever the prankster, he answered her queries with false answers three times. She persisted though, and finally, when his "soul was vexed to death," he said "A razor has never come upon my head. . . . If I be shaved, then my strength will leave me, and I shall become weak, and be like any other man." Delilah told the Philistines what she had learned, and they came to her chambers with silver for her reward, and soldiers to ensure Samson's downfall. Thus, while the biblical Hercules slept on her knees, seven locks were cut from his hair (Judges 16:16–17).

Valerio Castello's *Samson and Delilah* was inspired by grand opera, the most popular art form of the artist's day. Indeed 17th-century viewers of this life-sized work would have felt privileged to enjoy front-row balcony seats for this great moment of tragedy. Though 17th-century opera did not use spotlights, the artist manages to bathe Delilah's hand and bosom and Samson's biceps in a special glow. The beautiful vamp hushes the Philistine soldiers as though she is a soprano singing a lullaby, while the Nazarine's noble profile rests in adoring rapture on the red fabric of her lap. The barber in red stands back, an arm's length away from the slumbering giant, remembering the bruises that Samson had

inflicted on his enemies in other days. His scissors are an odd, four-blade device, but they do the job.

Valerio Castello was primarily a fresco painter. The medium, which calls for an artist to lay paint on wet plaster, would have given him considerable practice at making images with broad, sure, and fast sweeps of his brush, for large sections of such a work must be completed before the day's application of plaster dries. In Delilah's golden yellow shawl and white underblouse, one can see the artist's spectacular fresco technique transferred to oil painting. These areas are created out of only a very few long, loose marks of the brush. When viewed up close the strokes can easily be counted, but at a distance they give the impression of gossamer cloth. Valerio's virtuosity is as showy as Samson and Delilah are handsome. One wonders what other works this appealing Italian artist might have painted and what fame he might have achieved had he lived beyond his 34th year.

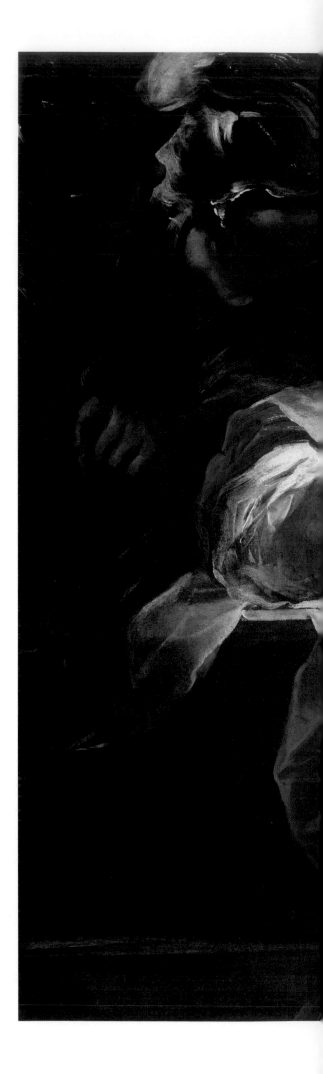

Samson and Delilah
VALERIO CASTELLO, Italian, 1625–1659

On loan from the collection of Mr. Channing Blake to the Museum of Fine Arts, Springfield, Massachusetts. Oil on canvas, 46 1/8 x 57 3/4 in.

The Blinding of Samson

REMBRANDT VAN RIJN, Dutch, 1606–1669

Städelsches Kunstinstitut, Frankfurt-am-Main. Oil on canvas,
92 7/8 x 118 7/8 in.

The Blinding of Samson

After Delilah discovered the secret of Samson's strength, she brought the Philistines into the Israelite's sleeping presence, and arranged for his locks to be trimmed. Then she woke him and watched as his enemies gouged out his eyes (Judges 16:21).

In *The Blinding of Samson*, Rembrandt captured this horrific event with a greater sense of realism than had ever been brought to the subject before. Not until 1907, when Lovis Corinth rendered *The Arrest and Blinding of Samson*, did another artist rival the 17th-century master in expressing the terrible nature of this bibilical story.

In the earlier version, Rembrandt provides brilliant light from an undisclosed source to silhouette the shears in the fleeing Delilah's hand. She looks over her shoulder with fascination and delight as an armored soldier plunges a serpentine dagger into Samson's right eye. His left eye is imperiled by another Philistine who readies his lance. As Samson feels the searing pain of steel enter his head, he grits his teeth, and his right foot lurches up uncontrollably toward Delilah. It is the first pain the hero has ever felt. The artist offers the viewer no relief from the horror of this instant, no glimmer of hope that Samson will eventually be saved or that the Philistines will perish. It is, quite simply, a gruesome painting about man's inhumanity to man. *The Blinding of Samson* stands alone in the great 17th-century Dutch master's oeuvre. He painted no other works of such violence. In fact, he painted *Samson* during the same year in which he worked on a related subject of utter tenderness, *Tobias Healing His Father's Blindness*.

It is also worth noting that he painted the picture for Constantijn Huygens, the most powerful and one of the best educated men in Holland. As secretary to the Stadtholder, Prince Frederick Henry of Orange, he held a position akin to that of lieutenant governor. In 1630, on behalf of the Prince, he commissioned Rembrandt to paint five large canvases on the subject of the Passion of Jesus. In gratitude, the artist gave him the sensational, life-sized *Samson* for his large, new house in The Hague. Along with it went a letter of instructions to "hang this piece in a strong light and so that one can stand at a distance from it, then it will sparkle at its best." While Huygens' letters attest to his taste for the horrific in art, there is no record of his reaction to Rembrandt's savage biblical "martyrdom."

Two hundred and seventy-one years later, the German artist Lovis Corinth based *The Arrest and Blinding of Samson* on Rembrandt's work. Indeed, all of the major elements in the two pictures are the same. Corinth, however, crowds the story into a vertical format, bringing together in a tight circle all of the figures that surround Samson. While Rembrandt wanted to put some distance between the protagonist and his captors to suggest their fear of the mighty Hebrew—hence his horizontal composition—Corinth's Philistines have no such concerns. They are driven by sadistic impulses, like frenzied savages. They have not blinded Samson yet, and the only blood in the scene is from the eye socket of the cringing figure in the foreground, downed as Samson's bed collapses. Corinth's signature appears on the blade of this poor fellow's broken knife near his hand.

Fascinated by Old Testament temptresses, Corinth presents Delilah in the nude; he treated other biblical seductresses in like fashion later in his career. Samson is also nude. Corinth hopes in this way to make the legendary lovers more human and vulnerable than they seem in Rembrandt's painting, and thus their story more believable. Certainly, the torture of Samson is more vivid as we see his flesh pummeled and bruised. The voluptuous body of the seductress is exactly the same color as that of the men under her gaze, and thus not very conspicuous. Only the gray-haired man under Samson's thigh seems to notice her, and he is no doubt calling to her for help as she flees the scene. Corinth does not allow the viewer to dwell on Delilah, either. Every compositional element brings the eye from her to the face of Samson. That is Rembrandt's intent as well. Thus the *link* between the pair, in both works, supports the theme that love blinds—and, alas, in Samson's case, that was literally true.

The Arrest and Blinding of Samson
LOVIS CORINTH, German, 1858–1925
Landesmuseum, Mainz, Germany. Oil on canvas, 78 x 68 in.

Samson Turning the Millstone
GEORGES ROUAULT, French, 1871–1958

Museum Purchase with Mr. and Mrs. George Gard de Sylva
Funds, Los Angeles County Museum of Art. Oil on canvas,
57 3/4 x 44 7/8 in.

The Ordeal of Samson

Of all the episodes in the story of
Samson, the one described in the
21st verse of the 16th chapter of Judges is
the most pathetic. After the Philistines
blinded the biblical Hercules, they took
him to Gaza, where they "bound him with
bronze fetters, and he ground at the mill in
the prison." There is no mention of a plan
of escape, a thirst for vengeance, or a willingness to take madcap risks. There is
nothing, in short, that would remind the
reader of the mighty Samson of old, the
hero who slew 1,000 of his enemies with
the jawbone of an ass.

The hero in his humiliating captivity is
the subject of Georges Rouault's *Samson*

Turning the Millstone, a work that clearly shows
the giant as a slave of his evil captors. The
Philistines whip and scorn him as he brave-
ly uses all of the remaining strength in his
lean body to move the huge millstone.
Unable to see their vile expressions, he
holds his head high and trudges his circular
route in dignity. Also unseen by him is a
woman in a seductive dress at the far left
side of the canvas. With her is the child
that she has brought to see the great lover-
hero. In the murky background of the dun-
geon, others also watch the once-great
Israelite in his misery.

In his youth, Georges Rouault was
apprenticed to a maker of stained glass.
Eventually he studied painting and, in fact,
was a student of Gustave Moreau when he
created *Samson Turning the Millstone*, While
the black outlines of stained glass design
would in time become a hallmark of his
style, they are not present in this early
work. Nor are the glowing colors of painted glass, another trademark of Rouault's
maturity. Although it is almost 5 feet tall,
Samson Turning the Millstone has more the
appearance of a drawing than a painting.
There is a strong linear quality to all of the
figures, particularly those of the spectators. Using only earth colors, and casting
the background in darkness, the artist
ensures that nothing will detract from the
humiliation of his central figure.

As a student, Rouault sought the Prix de
Rome scholarship, an annual prize that had
been the object of feverish competition
among French art students since its incep-
tion in 1666. Winning it not only enabled
a young artist to study in the Eternal City
for four years at the state's expense, it also
opened the door to official commissions.
To enter, one had to paint a canvas on a
given subject and submit it to a jury of
senior and usually highly opinionated
members of the French Academy of
Painters and Sculptors. In 1893 the subject was Samson, and this was the painting
that Rouault submitted. The jury did not
like it, probably because it lacked the slick
finish that they considered *de rigueur*, but
Moreau admired it sufficiently to sketch a
copy of it for himself.

The Levite and His Dead Concubine

Two of the 21 chapters of the Book of Judges were devoted to the horrifying story of an unnamed Levite and his concubine. According to Hebrew law, a marital bond existed between such a woman and her master (he was referred to as her husband), even though a concubine might be a slave. In this story, the Levite's concubine was unfaithful to her master and then escaped to the home of her father in Bethlehem. After four months, the Levite went "to speak kindly to her, and bring her back." He got along well with his father-in-law, but after a four-night visit he and the concubine set out for home. On their way, they found themselves in the square of a strange city as day was coming to an end. Although they were strangers, an old man insisted that they come to his house and they accepted his invitation. It was a decision they came to regret.

"As they were making their hearts merry," says the Book of Judges, "behold, the men of the city, base fellows, beset the house round about, beating on the door" (Judges 19:22). They asked the owner of the house to send his guest out to them, but the owner refused. He even offered, instead, his own daughter, stretching, it would seem, the rules of hospitality in an effort to protect his guests. The men continued to pound on the door until finally

the Levite and his concubine appeared at the threshold. Afraid for his life, he gave the woman to the rowdies, who repeatedly raped her and then left her at the doorstep. When the Levite rose in the morning, he found her there, "her hands on the threshold." He said to her, "Get up, let us be going." But there was no answer. She was dead.

In his prize-winning painting, *The Levite of Ephraim and His Dead Wife*, Jean-Jacques Henner shows the man arriving at his own home with the corpse of his concubine. According to the story (Judges 19:29–30), to vent his outrage over this murder, he dismembered her body, and sent parts of it to each of the 12 tribes of Israel, and the deed stirred up the whole nation—for the men who violated and killed her were of the tribe of Benjamin.

It is a brooding scene Henner presents to the viewer. The supine, marmoreal corpse of the concubine is veiled in a lugubrious haze. She is as spellbinding in her stillness as her story is in its violence and horror. The doleful Levite in his deep green robe seems to stare past her, focusing on his desire for vengeance.

The Levite of Ephraim and His Dead Wife earned Henner a Medal of Honor at the Salon of 1898. Although this was an unusual subject for a painting, the French knew the story through a prose poem by

Jean-Jacques Rousseau, written in 1762. Rousseau in his *Confessions* wrote that "If the Levite of Ephraim is not the best of my works, it will always be the most cherished."

Henner was from Alsace-Lorraine, a part of France that was lost to Germany after the Franco-Prussian War (1870/71). The artist saw in the Levite's loss and desire for retribution a parallel with the feelings of those whose homeland was dismembered. The painting may also serve as a comment on another significant event of the day, the scandalous Dreyfus Affair, in which an Alsatian Jew, Army Capt. Alfred Dreyfus, was convicted of treason on forged evidence and sent to Devil's Island. This affair, with its anti-Semitic overtones, may well have taxed the artist's patriotic loyalties.

The Levite of Ephraim and His Dead Wife
JEAN-JACQUES HENNER, French, 1829–1905

Collection of Mr. and Mrs. Joseph M. Tanenbaum, Toronto. Oil on canvas, 35½ x 65 ⅛ in.

Ruth and Naomi

The painting *Ruth and Naomi* by the relatively unknown Dutch artist Willem Drost introspectively depicts the young Moabite widow as she utters some of the most famous words in the Bible to her Israelite mother-in-law: "Where you go I will go, and where you lodge I will lodge; your people shall be my people, and your God my God" (Ruth 1:16).

The events leading up to this touching moment began a decade earlier when a famine drove Naomi, her husband, and their two sons from their home in Bethlehem to find food across the River Jordan in the foreign but fertile land of Moab. There the sons married local women, one of whom was Ruth. Naomi's husband died, and within a decade her sons died too. So she decided to leave her beloved daughters-in-law and return to Bethlehem. It took some arguing but finally one of the young women was persuaded to stay in Moab. Nothing, however, could disuade Ruth from accompanying her mother-in-law to her homeland.

The unselfish and even reckless faithfulness that Ruth showed Naomi inspired many artists over the centuries, but none of their depictions is as full of reflective melancholy as this version by Drost. Living in Holland, a Protestant country surrounded by states that were its religious and political enemies, may have helped the artist to understand the tensions between the Israelites and the Moabites (the descendents of Lot). In fact, the former were in constant fear of their children embracing the latter's pantheism, especially the sensuous and seductive rites of worship associated with the fertility god Baal. In turn, the Moabites considered their small but fertile land under threat from the Israelites. In times of famine, the two peoples forgot their differences, but in Ruth and Naomi's day the older woman was probably right in deciding to return to her homeland and in urging her daughter-in-law to stay with her own people.

In Drost's painting, Naomi is dressed for travel. She carries a large flask filled with water, and a drinking cup is suspended from her arm. Her golden yellow cloak is richly trimmed in metallic gold, as is the extravagant costume worn by Ruth. Drost, who embraced his teacher Rembrandt's

taste for exotic clothing, probably bought these garments or borrowed them from someone who asserted their biblical authenticity. Whether the costumes are genuine or not, they rather enhance the tender and deeply felt exchange that is at the heart of the picture. The artist, who was a fine portrait painter, captures the beauty of the biblical text in the faces of the two heroines, and in the hand of Naomi, which turns, as the older woman recognizes Ruth's devotion, from a farewell embrace to a sign of blessing.

Ruth and Naomi

WILLEM DROST, Dutch, active 1652–1680

Ashmolean Museum, Oxford. Oil on canvas,
34 3/4 x 27 1/2 in.

Ruth and Boaz

Ruth and Naomi arrived in Bethlehem at the start of the barley harvest. With no means of support, the young widow volunteered to glean in the fields, knowing that the job would provide sufficient food for herself and her mother-in-law. Her great beauty soon caught the eye of Boaz, a rich kinsman of Naomi's late husband. In time, she and Boaz married and had a child, at whose birth the midwives said to Naomi, "He shall be to you a restorer of life and a nourisher of your old age; for your daughter-in-law who loves you, who is more to you than seven sons, has born him." Naomi nursed the child, named Obed, and he became the father of Jesse and the grandfather of David (Ruth 1:22–4:17).

In his masterpiece *Harvesters Resting*, Jean-François Millet, the great French painter of peasants, shows Boaz asking Ruth to join his reapers for lunch. It is an early moment in the couple's courtship, and Ruth doesn't yet know any of her coworkers. She seems reluctant to join the strangers, but receives encouragement at least from Boaz's dog. Nearby the workers are already at rest. By showing the peasants at leisure instead of in backbreaking work, Millet can focus on the dignity of these men and women who had become forgotten in an increasingly urbanized France. He links the two groups of figures through Boaz's gesture of invitation, and through the use of color: the blues in Ruth's costume and the red-browns and yellows of Boaz's clothing find their counterparts in the laborers' trousers, skirts, headgear, and sleeve coverings. The only contrast to these soft tones is the weathered white of the harvesters' shirts. All the figures are enveloped in a haze of warm pinkish yellow that rises in warm weather from the crop and its dust.

Millet desired more than anything else "to make pictures that mattered," and this painting was the most ambitious of his career. Following the precepts of the academic tradition, he prepared the composition in a laborious and detailed way.

Hundreds of drawings were made to determine the placement of figures, the pose and musculature of each, their gestures and facial expressions, and the drape and details of their costumes. In other drawings he experimented with various landscape settings, and numerous colored sketches led to the final palette. Some of these preparatory works date from as early as 1847. Millet entered the finished painting in the official art exhibition of 1853, where it earned a second-class medal. One widely read critic heralded the painting as "the poetry and the majesty of the populace," while calling the figures "superbly ugly, brutal, and primitive."

According to the laws of Moses, "When you reap the harvest of your land, you shall not reap your field to its very border, neither shall you gather the gleanings after your harvest." A similar law pertained to the vineyard and another to the olive grove. These leavings—or gleanings—were reserved "for the poor and the sojourner," "the fatherless and the widow" (Leviticus 19:9; Deuteronomy 24:21). In France, the poor and the aged were traditionally allowed the gleanings. But in the 19th century, even the peasantry were in need of these communal privileges as large landowners expanded their holdings and crowded them out of the small plots they had long worked for themselves. When Millet was active as a painter of peasant life, the numbers of desperately poor rose dramatically, and at harvest time they wandered the countryside, competing with local peasants for the gleanings. Millet hoped to bring attention to their plight by recalling in this great work that the virtuous Ruth was once a gleaner.

Harvesters Resting (Ruth and Boaz)

JEAN-FRANÇOIS MILLET, French, 1814–1875

Bequest of Mrs. Martin Brimmer, Museum of Fine Arts, Boston. Oil on canvas, 26 1/2 x 47 1/8 in.

David and Goliath

D avid, the seventh and last son of Jesse, was arguably the greatest hero of the Old Testament. To be sure, the tale of his life took Jewish narrative art to its zenith, and some of the highest moments in painting—from Byzantine times to the 19th century—were inspired by his story.

The first mention of David in the Holy Scriptures offered a physical description of the lad: "he was ruddy, had beautiful eyes, and was handsome" (I Samuel 16:12). He was a shepherd.

Florentines had adopted the Hebrew as their symbol, and no episode from his life better epitomized their view of themselves than that of the young, beautiful shepherd battling and killing the gigantic Philistine, Goliath. In *The Youthful David*, painted on leather shaped as a shield, Andrea del Castagno, one of the great masters of Renaissance painting, shows the stalwart youth as he is about to loose a smooth stone from his sling. He also shows the result of the shot, in the bloody head of Goliath lying between David's feet.

Georgio Vasari, the 16th-century chronicler of the lives of Italian artists, said that Andrea "excels in showing movement in his figures." Certainly, his *David* supports that opinion. The youth's arm is raised, not for show, nor as a victory gesture, but to balance the spin of his athletic body as the backward thrust of the sling is about to change into a forward propulsion. Vasari also commented on the disquieting and grave expressions of the faces in Andrea's works. Here too *David* provides a case in point, as the lad looks totally absorbed in his mission. His nervous energy is suggested by the flying hair and the splayed fingers, and this quality is, in turn, echoed in the quick and darting movement of the clouds across the sky. The artist did not have to show exaggerated musculature to indicate David's strength. By placing the lad's feet toward the edges of the narrow end of the shield, the opposing angles create a dynamic that suggests power.

The Youthful David

ANDREA DEL CASTAGNO, Italian, 1417/19–1457

Widener Collection, National Gallery of Art, Washington,
D.C. Leather on wood panel, 45 1/2 x 30 1/4 to 16 1/8 in.

David's Triumph

After he killed the giant warrior Goliath, the shepherd boy David emerged as a full-blown national hero. Standing before King Saul and the royal court, Goliath's head in his hand, he reminded the ruler that he was "the son of your servant Jesse the Bethlehemite." Jonathan, the King's son and chief commander, was deeply moved and impressed by the nobility of the lad. In the poetic words of the Bible, "the soul of Jonathan was knit to the soul of David, and Jonathan loved him as his own soul." After the defeat of the Philistines, King Saul returned to Jerusalem in triumph. Women came from all the cities and towns of Israel to welcome their King and their loved ones back from battle. They were a merry lot, singing "songs of joy," playing musical instruments, and dancing (1 Samuel 17:54; 18:6–9). David the great hero enjoyed his share of praise as well. In fact, Saul heard the women singing, "Saul has slain his thousands, and David his ten thousands." These words so angered the King that he "eyed David from that day on" (1 Samuel 18:7–9).

Cima da Conegliano, the Italian Renaissance painter, and Nicolas Poussin, the leading figure of French Classicism, choose two very different moments from David's life in the wake of his triumph over Goliath. Cima, in his lovely small painting *David and Jonathan*, shows the two young men alone together after David's meeting with Saul. A lush setting provides the backdrop for this budding friendship, and a small amphitheater of golden earth lies beneath the young men's feet. Along with Goliath's head, which David carries as a trophy, he also wields the giant's sword. This weapon symbolizes the Philistines' former military superiority over the Israelites—prior to David's intervention, that is—a superiority due largely to the Philistine's monopoly on forged iron. David himself is not given extraordinary attributes. In fact, his elaborate clothing diminishes him in stature, making him appear very young and almost doll-like. And Jonathan is not dressed as a prince. Except for the startling head that faces the

David and Jonathan
CIMA DA CONEGLIANO, Italian, 1460(?)–1517/18(?)
The National Gallery, London. Oil on wood panel, 15⅝ x 15¼ in.

viewer directly, these two could be any young soldiers on their way home from battle.

By contrast to Cima's glimpse into David's private life, Poussin's *The Triumph of David* captures the young hero's public welcome into Jerusalem. Some writers have suggested that the figure in the turban on the far right side is Saul. Whoever he is, he and his companions are animatedly discussing young David's marksmanship. One of them points to his own forehead as he recalls the remarkable shot that felled Goliath. David himself is center stage. With skimpy sandals, a brief red tunic, and almost no accessories, except for a pouch around his waist, he nevertheless seems far more heroic than the David in Cima's painting. Certainly, he stands out from the crowd that encircles him, their eyes riveted on his gruesome trophy. The mother in a lime green dress and red mantle in the foreground shows her small child the giant's head. The boy is frightened, but the mother smiles, telling him perhaps that Goliath was the champion of the enemy his father had fought.

Inspired by ancient Roman reliefs of great parades for heroes, Poussin stages his triumphal march before the high porch of a temple similar to that of Jupiter Capitolinus in Rome. Though the architectural style is consistent with the drapery on the figures, it postdates the age of David by almost five centuries. Seventeenth-century Europeans were impressed by the artist's carefully researched and archaeologically correct depictions of antiquity and did not quibble about exact dates. Apparently the renowned filmmaker Cecil B. De Mille was also impressed, for he used Poussin's reconstructions as source material for some of the sets in his epics. In Cima's time, by contrast, the science of archaeology was still rudimentary. He thus depended more on fancy than fact for his costumes and landscape.

The Triumph of David

NICOLAS POUSSIN, French, 1594–1665

Dulwich Picture Gallery, London. Oil on canvas,
46 5/8 x 58 3/8 in.

The Death of Saul

Pieter Bruegel's incredibly detailed painting *The Suicide of Saul* provides viewers with an overview of the routing of the Israelites by the Philistines, an event described in the last verses of the First Book of Samuel. Three of Saul's sons died in the battle, including the upright and loyal Jonathan. Saul himself was badly wounded by the Philistine archers. Not wishing to be captured by the cruel foe, the King asked his faithful armor bearer to kill him with his sword. When the man refused, Saul fell upon his own weapon. His frightened servant followed suit.

In Bruegel's interpretation of the story, the spears of the victorious Philistines are upright, their archers standing in orderly ranks before piles of dead and wounded. The routed troops of Saul are identified by waves of tilting spears filling the valley and ascending the forested slope, where the vanquished seek places to hide. Off to the left are King Saul and his armor bearer, ignominiously dead. The only signs of the former's royalty are the fleur-de-lis that decorate his helmet and the quality of the armor that encases his still-warm body. Below him, Philistines are following a narrow path to behead him and cart his carcass away.

The Suicide of Saul
PIETER BRUEGEL THE ELDER, Flemish, ca. 1525–1569
Kunsthistorisches Museum, Vienna. Oil on wood panel,
13 x 21 1/2 in.

David Dances Before the Ark of the Covenant

JAN DE BRAY, Dutch, 1627–1691

Gift of Mrs. Joseph Wolf, Evansville Museum of Arts and Science, Indiana. Oil on canvas, 46 x 69 in.

David Dancing Before the Lord

Part of the reason that David captured the imagination of so many generations of artists was that he embodied such a range of universal ideals of manhood: he was a warrior, a poet, a musician, a lover, and a statesman. It is David the musician that Jan de Bray acknowledges in *David Dances Before the Ark of the Covenant*. A number of biblical stories mentioned the ruler's prowess with a harp, but none evoked an image as oddly disquieting as this one.

After David became King of Israel and moved his capital to Jerusalem, he tried to serve as an example of religious devotion to his people, in contrast to his predecessor, Saul, who had paid little attention to spiritual matters. Among other things, David organized a national celebration around the relocation of the Ark of the Covenant to Jerusalem. On this auspicious occasion, horns sounded and there was singing. Dressed in the traditional linen robe of a priest, "David danced before the Lord with all his might." Because he performed in front of unmarried girls, his behavior infuriated one of his wives, Michal, the daughter of Saul. Ignoring her wrath, David continued to "make merry before the Lord." For her disrespect toward the sacred ceremony, Michal was cursed with barrenness for the rest of her life (2 Samuel 6:15–23).

Dutch artists knew the Old Testament well, as did their countrymen, if the frequent appearance of biblical names on 17th-century baptismal records is any indication. Thus, they would have understood Jan de Bray's introduction of stringed instruments into the Ark celebration—even though the Bible only mentioned horns— as a reference to David's prowess with a harp. Indeed, the artist shows the musical monarch strumming his instrument while he energeticaliy stomps his feet to the rhythm of a timbrel player. The members of his party seem to be enjoying the tune, except Michal, who stares pointedly at her husband from the window in the upper left corner of the canvas.

De Bray was primarily a portrait painter, but in *David Dances Before the Ark of the Covenant* he shows his mastery of the figure in action. Particularly noteworthy is his rendering of the story's protagonist, whose right foot is raised high in the flat-footed dance of an ordinary peasant. His joyful abandon stands in contrast to the utter seriousness of the other celebrants, whose looks of concentration are convincingly captured by de Bray. Through body language and facial expression, the artist also conveys the twin viewpoints of the story: David's belief that his dancing is pleasing to God, and Michal's revulsion at its earthiness.

Bathsheba at Her Bath

HANS MEMLING, Flemish, 1433–1494

Staatsgalerie, Stuttgart. Oil and tempera on wood panel, 74 1/2 x 32 15/16 in.

Bathsheba at Her Bath

As related in the 11th chapter of the Second Book of Samuel, King David fell in love with Bathsheba when he spied her bathing and had her brought to his palace as his lover. When she became pregnant, David recalled her husband Uriah, a Hittite soldier who was off fighting in one of his wars, assuming that on his return home he would have marital relations with his wife and draw the logical conclusion when he discovered her condition. But Uriah refused to go home while his colleagues were in battle. David then arranged for him to be assigned to the front lines where he was killed. Thereafter the King married Bathsheba, and she gave birth to a son. But the child died because God was displeased by David's callous manipulations.

Although artists usually show David as an ancient seducing a bathing beauty, he was probably close to 40 years of age when he first saw Bathsheba. He had already married at least six times, had bedded numerous concubines, and had fathered no less than nine legitimate sons. Given his extensive harem, Bathsheba must have been stunning. The opportunity to paint this beautiful naked woman and to explore the theme of seduction is what repeatedly drew artists to the tale.

Hans Memling, the most successful painter in the great Flemish trading city of Bruges during the second half of the 15th century, specialized in portraits and religious subjects. On only a few occasions did he have the excuse to paint female nudity. In *Bathsheba at Her Bath*, Memling decides to show the young matron in an upper-class bedroom, rising from a nap, and stepping out of her nightgown. The figure reveals the long limbs and rounded belly that were the standards of female beauty throughout the 15th century. Only the viewer can see her nakedness, for her maid modestly averts her eyes and King David, way off in the background, cannot see her yet. He will have plenty of time to study her figure, however, for the tiny jug at her feet contains all the wash water at her disposal and thus a bath is likely to take a while. Near the jug and washpan is a little dog, an ironic symbol of Bathsheba's marital fidelity.

Amnon and Tamar

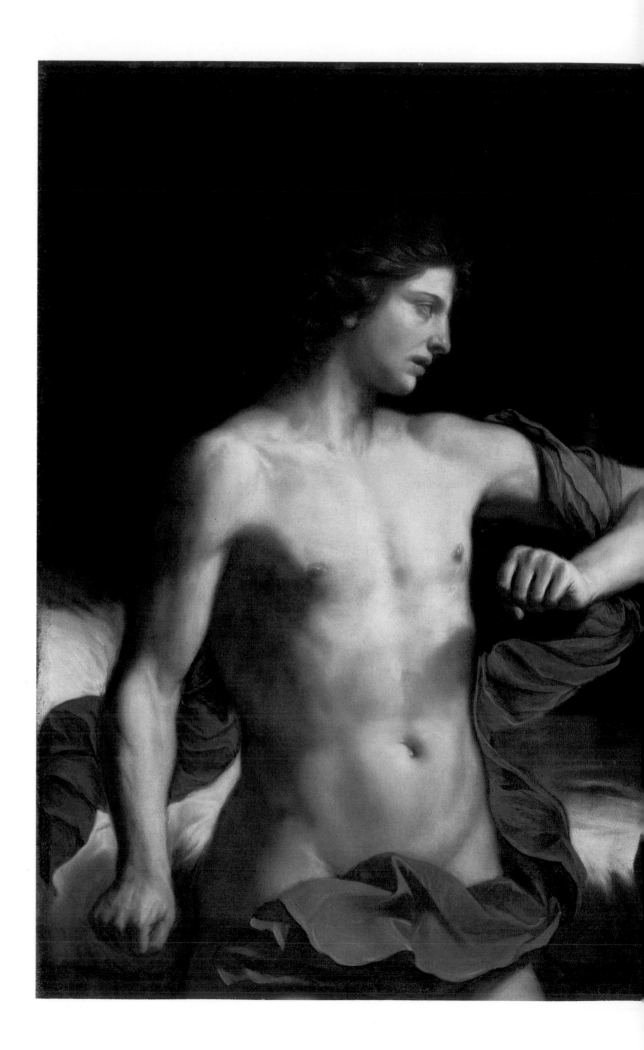

artin Luther said that "The Greek tragedies are not to be compared with the history of David. . . .No miserable man ever surpassed him." For the most part, however, the King led a charmed life, but he did suffer at the hands of his children. The Bible dwells on stories about three of them, Amnon, the King's eldest son; Tamar, his beautiful daughter by another wife; and Absalom, Tamar's full brother. Two of these children are featured in Guercino's *Amnon and Tamar.* As the white linen of the bed and the near-nudity of the figures suggests, it is a painting about incest.

Amnon was in love with his half-sister Tamar and was prompted by his cousin and close friend Jonadab to seduce her. Feigning illness, he asked his father to send Tamar to nurse him and bake cakes for him. The King complied, but once she was in his house, Amnon raped her. When he was done, his lust turned to shame, and he sought to drive her from his sight. "No, my brother," she pleaded, "this wrong in sending me away is greater than the other which you did to me," suggesting that Amnon, having ruined her, was now responsible for her care. Amnon, however, was not an honorable man, and he was unmoved by her plight. Finally, the sobbing young woman ripped her garment, covered herself with ashes and fled. Thereafter, she "dwelt, a desolate woman, in her brother Absalom's house" (2 Samuel 13:15-–20). Two years later, in revenge for the rape of his sister, Absalom had Amnon murdered in the presence of all of David's children.

Amnon and Tamar by Guercino finds the siblings at the peak moment in the drama—that in which Tamar pleads with her brother for support. The Bible described her robe as long-sleeved, the

kind worn by all the virgin daughters of the King, but Guercino, apparently unfamiliar with the text, drapes her in a piece of mauve fabric. Amnon's nakedness is covered by a scarf of blue pigment derived from the lapis lazuli gemstone. There are no other colors in the painting, so all the viewer's attention is focused on the two figures, their body language, and the expressions on their faces. Amnon is particularly expressive, his hands balled up into fists, like those of a spoiled child.

Guercino paired this tragic and frightening image with his painting of Joseph and Potiphar's wife. Together, they spoke to the conduct expected of a moral man, with Amnon as the bad example and Joseph the good one. While the story of the latter appears frequently in art, the brutal tale of Amnon and Tamar found favor only occasionally, and then usually in court circles where it was used to instruct young princes on proper behavior.

Amnon and Tamar

GUERCINO (GIOVANNI FRANCESCO BARBIERI), Italian, 1591–1666

Patrons' Permanent Fund, National Gallery of Art, Washington, D.C. Oil on canvas, 48 3/4 x 62 1/8 in.

Esther and Mordecai

Mordecai, a Jew living in Persia, raised his orphaned cousin Esther as his own daughter. She grew into a great beauty, becoming one of the women in King Ahasuerus' harem, and later his Queen. Mordecai was a doorman at the palace. Because he refused to bow down to Haman, the highest of the princes and chief minister, he won the evil man's enmity. So great in fact was Haman's wrath that, when he discovered Mordecai's religion, he convinced the King to annihilate all of the Israelites in Persia's vast empire.

In *Esther and Mordecai*, the great Renaissance artist Andrea Mantegna depicts the defiant Jew showing the death edict to his adopted daughter, the Queen. "Our race will be wiped out," he seems to say. "I will be killed with the others, and so will you if your religion is discovered" (Esther 2, 3, and 4:1–9). That these dire events did not occur was solely due to Esther's intervention with Ahasuerus on the Israelites' behalf. That is the subject of the next painting in this book.

During the Renaissance, Esther came to be regarded as one of history's greatest heroines, and from then on she became the subject of many paintings, as well as poems, oratorios, operas, and plays. Mantegna chose to render his depiction of the heroine and her adopted father in grisaille, a most austere and exacting technique relying solely upon shades of gray. Often used to fake sculpture, grisaille requires the artist to exert a convincing control over light and dark, and to be aware of how monochromatic shades would translate into color in real life. Mantegna shows himself to be a master of the technique, going far beyond the mere presentation of convincing three-dimensionality to also capture the weights and textures of his subject's garments. Esther's robes are of light, sheer textiles, whereas Mordecai's are almost leathery and heavy.

By viewing the figures from below, the artist is able to show off his knowledge of foreshortening, a newly developed technique of which he was among the first masters. The low vantage point not only elevates Esther and Mordecai physically, it also implies that they are psychologically—and morally—elevated. Looking almost like sculptures on a high ledge, the figures are treated by the artist as heroes, noble figures to which one can justifiably look up.

Esther and Mordecai
ANDREA MANTEGNA, Italian, 1431–1506
Bequest of Mary M. Emery, Cincinnati Art Museum. Oil on canvas, 22 ¹/₈ x 19 ¹/₈ in.

sther decided to go to her husband, King Ahasuerus, and plead for her people, the Jews, who were being slaughtered under royal sanction. Her mission entailed great risk, for to approach the King's chambers without his invitation was to court death. So, before she went to Ahasuerus, she fasted for three days. So did all the Jews in the capital city of Susa. Finally, dressed in her royal robes, she made her way to the King's hall. When Ahasuerus saw her, he raised his golden scepter and motioned for her to enter. In *Queen Esther Pleads with Her Husband Ahasuerus for the Rescue of the Jewish People*, the German artist Hans Burgkmair the Elder shows her touching the top of the scepter, a gesture that is faithful to the biblical account of the story. Although she knew that her husband loved her—he had proved it by promising her anything she wanted, even half his kingdom—she proceeded cautiously with her plan, inviting Ahasuerus to dinner and asking him to bring Haman with him. After two nights of banqueting, she decided the time was finally right to reveal her religion to the King and to plead for her people. The plan worked. Ahasuerus rescinded the death warrants and ordered the execution of Haman, the author of the heinous edict. Appropriately, the evil prince was put to death on the gallows that he had built for his nemesis Mordecai, Esther's beloved cousin and protector.

Burgkmair, like his contemporary Albrecht Dürer, had visited Italy and brought back what he had learned to Germany. While Dürer imported ideals of Renaissance form and beauty, Burgkmair concentrated on elements of Renaissance design. Architectural details that he saw in the south abound in this painting and are integrated into a lavishly ornate composition through the use of linear perspective, another Italian import. The great open courts in the background—a feature of ancient Near Eastern architecture mentioned in the Bible—suggest the lavishness of Ahasuerus' palace. It did not matter to the citizens of Augsburg, where Burgkmair resided, that the arches, balustrades, and columns—the latter more like jewelry than architecture—do not remotely resemble the buildings of Susa, Persia's winter capital. It wasn't until 1852 and again in 1884–1886 that archaeological expeditions explored the site.

Though the lavish setting was designed to awe Burgkmair's audience, the artist also hoped that his painting would inspire viewers to follow the example of Esther, who put principles before all else, jeopardizing her position, her power, and her pampered life to speak out for her people and religion. It must have been difficult for many Germans to emulate the ways of Esther at the start of the Reformation. Augsburg, like Susa, was a place of enormous wealth. It was the home of Europe's richest and most powerful banking families, the Fuggers and the Welsers, and they were at their zenith when Burgkmair was active as the city's chief painter. Nonetheless many of the town's citizens did speak out for their religion. Indeed, in 1530, just two years after Burgkmair painted this work, the disciples of Martin Luther issued their first formal articles of faith in Augsburg.

Queen Esther Pleads with Her Husband Ahasuerus for the Rescue of the Jewish People

HANS BURGKMAIR THE ELDER, German, 1473–1531

Alte Pinakothek, Munich. Oil on wood panel, 40 1/8 x 60 15/16 in.

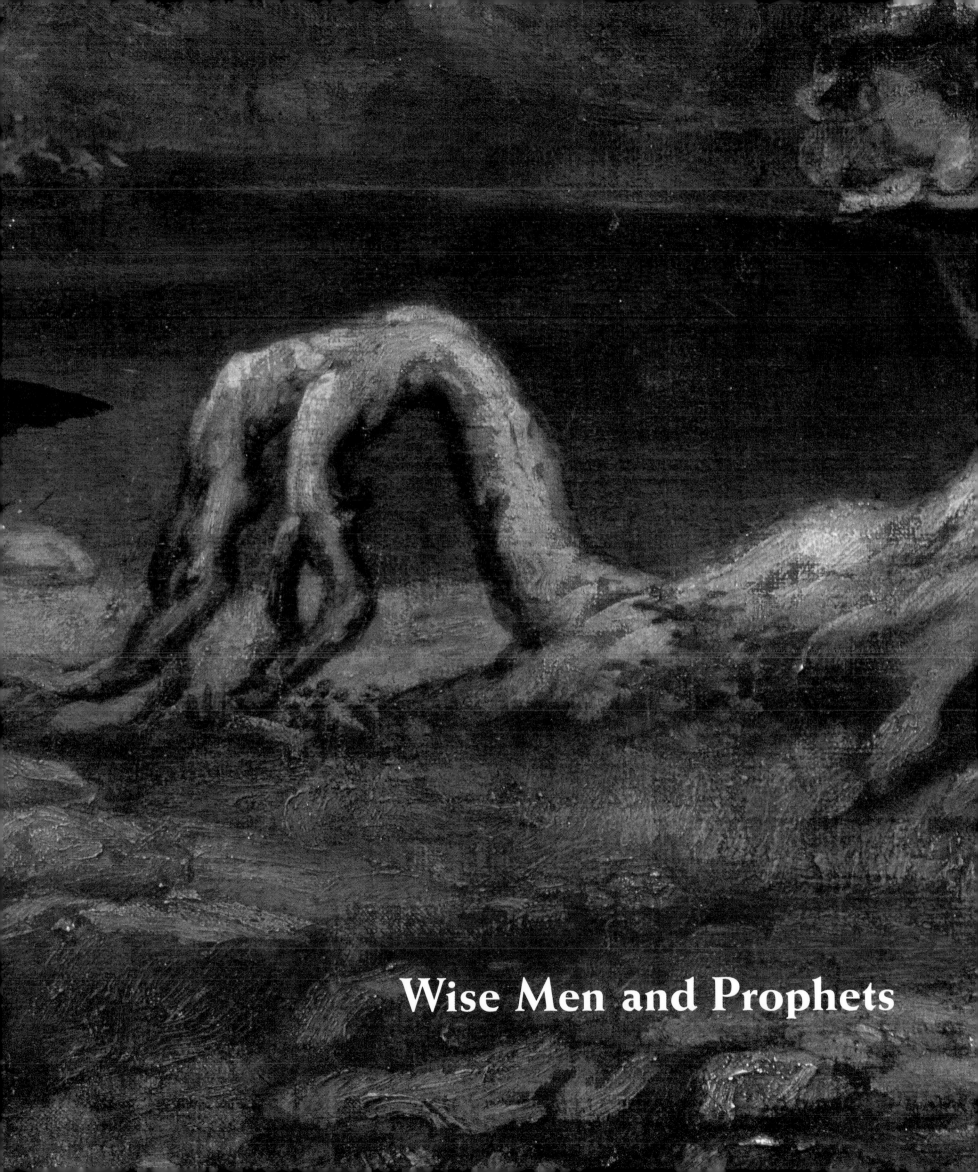

Wise Men and Prophets

Solomon, the son of David and Bathsheba, was celebrated for his wisdom. It was an endowment that he neither inherited nor learned from experience, but rather received as a gift from God. It happened early in his reign as King of Israel, when the Lord came to him in a dream, saying, "Ask what I shall give you." "I am but a little child; I do not know how to go out or come in," Solomon replied in a sincere and self-deprecating manner. "Give thy servant an understanding mind to govern thy people, that I may discern between good and evil" (I Kings 3:5–9). God was so pleased with this unselfish request that he granted Solomon wisdom, along with great riches and honor that he had not sought.

The King's new gift was soon put to the test when two harlots came to him with a problem to solve. The women lived in the same house and each had given birth to a son. During the night, one of the babies died when his mother rolled over onto him, so she callously replaced her dead baby with the other woman's child. The next morning, the second mother protested the exchange, but the cheating harlot would not relinquish the living child. When the case came before the King, he asked for a sword. "Divide the living child in two, and give half to the one and half to the other," he ordered. The cheating harlot accepted Solomon's ruling, but the other woman quickly relinquished her claim to the child, for she could not bear to see it die. Solomon knew then who the rightful mother was and awarded the baby to her (I Kings 3:23–28). From that day until the end of his long life, his people acknowledged the wisdom of their King.

In *The Judgment of Solomon*, Poussin creates an unusually symmetrical composition, one that is rich in moral solemnity, with the characters revealing their deeply felt emotions through broad gestures and facial expressions. Dominating the scene is the King. With his arms extended like the balance of a scale, he proclaims his dramatic solution to the case before him. A half-nude soldier wearing a helmet crowned by a large gold griffin (a protective symbol in ancient art) dangles the child in front of him with one hand as he unsheathes his long sword with the other. The false mother points to the soldier as she shouts her assent to Solomon's solution, while the other woman begs the monarch to spare her child, not knowing that the boy will soon be returned to her embrace.

Poussin's depiction of a great marble hall offers an appropriate backdrop to this story, for Solomon preferred to lavish money on the temple, his palace, and the state's public buildings rather than spend it on military campaigns as his father had done. The high dais on which he sits resembles an ancient wellhead, metaphorically suggesting that Solomon was the font of God's wisdom. Poussin was pleased with this painting, considering it his best work.

The Judgment of Solomon
NICOLAS POUSSIN, French, 1594–1665
Musée du Louvre, Paris. Oil on canvas, 39 3/8 x 59 in.

PRECEDING PAGES

ALLSTON: *Elijah in the Desert* (detail)

Solomon and Sheba

The Queen of Sheba went unnamed in the Bible, but by tradition she was known as Balkis and was very likely the ruler of the trading peoples of southern Arabia and the nearby coast of Ethiopia. When she learned of Solomon's wealth, she sought to establish a trade relationship between their peoples, so she brought him gold and samples of the spices, gems, and rare woods that her caravan masters got from Africa, India, and the East. He in turn showed her his wealth. She also tested him with questions, and "told him all that was on her mind," after which she concluded that he was wiser, richer, and far greater than his legend (l Kings 10:1–13).

For ages writers have speculated on the nature of the relationship between this royal pair and have pondered the Bible's meaning when it says that Soloman gave her "all that she desired." Because she was an exotic, probably the King's lover, and, most importantly, a convert to Judaism, the Queen of Sheba became a popular figure in religious art. During the Middle Ages, for example, she was frequently chosen to grace the facades of imposing cathedrals along with other great Jewish and Christian monarchs. Somewhat later, in around 1435, the German-Swiss artist Konrad Witz made her the subject of a panel painting called *The Queen of Sheba Before Solomon*.

Witz creates a youthful couple, with the King barely able to hold his head erect under the weight of his jewel-studded red felt hat. The shimmering skirt of his black satin gown forms folds independent of the anatomy beneath it, suggesting a body of little substance. Witz makes the Queen Caucasian rather than black, as the prevailing tradition maintained. She looks around in awe at the richly tooled gold interior, realizing that it far outshines the gifts the two monarchs have presented to one another. The theme of the altarpiece from which this painting comes is redemption. Hence, what is most important in this work is the Queen's stature as convert, one who saw the surrounding wealth as God's way of blessing Solomon for his wisdom and goodness.

Sheba is a great and elegant beauty in Edward John Poynter's *The Visit of the Queen of Sheba to King Solomon*, painted in around 1885. As with Poynter's contemporaries, the poets Robert Browning (*Solomon and Balkis*, 1883) and William Butler Yeats (*Solomon to Sheba*, 1919), the artist is clearly more interested in exploring the physical attraction between the two than he is in depicting Sheba's spiritual awakening. The revival of interest in this royal beauty among British artists and writers during the latter part of the 19th century was no doubt prompted by the popularity of their own Queen, Victoria, and by the desire to find historical precedents for her virtues and the wealth of the British Empire under her rule.

The late 19th century also saw a sharply increased interest in Solomon sparked by archaeologists' newly created reconstructions of antique monuments. Persepolis, the Great Hall of Columns at Karnak, and Solomon's Temple were among the most popular reconstructions, and flocks of people came to see the fascinating miniature models of them. Poynter himself designed a reconstruction of the reception room in Solomon's palace, the "Hall of the Throne" mentioned in First Kings. He even commissioned a model of it to guide him in the execution of this huge painting. Pillars and beams made of cedars of Lebanon, capitals of bronze modeled by one Hiram, from Tyre, and golden overlays are specifications mentioned in the Bible, as are the 12 lions flanking the stairs that lead to the throne (l Kings 10:20). By his unswerving attention to fact and detail, Poynter restored history painting in England to a place of importance.

The Queen of Sheba before Solomon
KONRAD WITZ, German, ca. 1400–1444/6
Gemaldegalerie Berlin-Dahlem. Oil on wood panel,
40 1/8 x 60 15/16 in.

FOLLOWING PAGES
The Visit of the Queen of Sheba To King Solomon
SIR EDWARD JOHN POYNTER, English, 1836–1919
Art Gallery of New South Wales, Sydney. Oil on canvas,
91 1/2 x 136 11/16 in

Elijah in the Desert

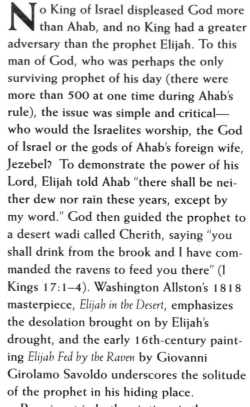

No King of Israel displeased God more than Ahab, and no King had a greater adversary than the prophet Elijah. To this man of God, who was perhaps the only surviving prophet of his day (there were more than 500 at one time during Ahab's rule), the issue was simple and critical—who would the Israelites worship, the God of Israel or the gods of Ahab's foreign wife, Jezebel? To demonstrate the power of his Lord, Elijah told Ahab "there shall be neither dew nor rain these years, except by my word." God then guided the prophet to a desert wadi called Cherith, saying "you shall drink from the brook and I have commanded the ravens to feed you there" (1 Kings 17:1–4). Washington Allston's 1818 masterpiece, *Elijah in the Desert*, emphasizes the desolation brought on by Elijah's drought, and the early 16th-century painting *Elijah Fed by the Raven* by Giovanni Girolamo Savoldo underscores the solitude of the prophet in his hiding place.

Prominent in both paintings is the raven, who is perched near Elijah's shoulder in the Italian work, and in two places in Allston's painting—high on the branch of a dead tree and within reach of the kneeling prophet. At first glance, the raven is an odd choice for God's mission, because, as a carnivore, it was listed with the unclean animals in Mosaic law. In addition, Aesop, who ranked with the authors of the Bible in importance during Savoldo's lifetime, offered a fable that found the raven an outcast among other birds because of its false heart. But the Book of Job and Psalms mention the raven as a creature under God's special care (Job 38:41; Psalm 147:9). Regardless, this outcast brought meat and bread to the hermit Elijah every

Elijah Fed by the Raven

GIOVANNI GIROLAMO SAVOLDO, Italian, ca. 1480–after 1548

Samuel H. Kress Collection, National Gallery of Art, Washington, D.C. Transferred from wood panel to canvas, 66 1/8 x 53 3/8 in.

Elijah in the Desert
WASHINGTON ALLSTON, American, 1779–1843
Gift of Mrs. Samuel Hooper and Miss Alice Hooper, Museum of Fine Arts, Boston. Oil on canvas, 48 3/4 x 72 1/2 in.

morning and every evening and seems to have been the prophet's sole companion until the brook went dry.

In the huge dead trees in the center of his canvas, Washington Allston symbolizes the great drought, which lasted for three years. They stand in contrast to the life-giving brook with its flowing waterfalls, a sign of the favor that Elijah found in God. Man's ability to coexist with nature, even as he is dwarfed by it, was a recurring theme in 18th-century art and literature. By combining this concern with the story of a biblical hero, Allston satisfied his desire to create "Old Master" paintings on grand themes. After enjoying great success in London, he returned to America, his native land, with this haunting work in hand. It eventually found its way into the Museum of Fine Arts in Boston, as the first accession of that great gallery.

Allston shows Elijah on his knees, praying for God to help him defeat the forces of Ahab and Jezebel. In Savoldo's work, the prophet turns to the raven, as though for inspiration. This motif has its equivalent in New Testament art, where Gospel writers frequently look to the Dove of the Holy Spirit for guidance. The connection of Elijah with New Testament figures is not fanciful. According to the Bible, the prophet never died. He was taken into heaven by a fiery chariot, whose horses were propelled by a whirlwind. All four of the Gospel writers recounted that he once appeared before Jesus with Moses and the three of them had a conversation. A strict order of Christian friars called the Carmelites built a monastery on Mount Carmel to commemorate Elijah's victory over the priests of Ahab and Jezebel. This order's devotion to Elijah, which in time spread throughout Europe, led to numerous art commissions featuring the prophet.

Elijah Restoring the Widow's Son

Elijah Restoring the Widow's Son
FORD MADOX BROWN, English, 1821–1893
Victoria and Albert Museum, London. Watercolor,
36 ³/₄ x 23 ⁷/₈ in.

The brook Cherith dried up, but Elijah continued to receive divine protection. With no available water, however, he was instructed by the Lord to go to a town called Zare-phath. It was a long distance from the wadi, but it was also far from Elijah's enemies. A widow there was to feed him. After he arrived on her doorstep, her only provisions—a small handful of meal in a jar and a little oil in a cruet—never ran out. The widow had a young son, and while Elijah was a guest in her house the child fell severely ill and stopped breathing. The widow accused the prophet of bringing this bad luck to her house, but Elijah ignored her, taking the still child to an upper room and praying over the lad until his health was restored.

Ford Madox Brown, a meticulous Victorian artist, managed to crowd his painting *Elijah Restoring the Widow's Son* with numerous details without distracting from the power of its narrative. The child is wrapped in funeral linens, and the flowers that were placed on his head and in his hands for his farewell to life now symbolize his resurrection. As the prophet makes his way down the massive stone steps, his boldly embroidered gray wool cloak flies up behind him, as if it has an energy of its own. "See, your son lives," Elijah says to the widow as he brings the boy back down from the upper room. "Now I know . . . that the word of the Lord in your mouth is truth," the widow responds, recognizing the power of God in her guest and thanking him on her knees (I Kings 17:8–24).

The artist has marked the house as a religious one with a Hebrew inscription from Deuteronomy framing the door: "The Lord our God is one Lord; and you shall love the Lord your God with all your heart, and with all your soul, and with all your might" (Deuteronomy 6:4). He also indicates that it is an efficient home through myriad still-life details, including the tidy strand of garlic, the whisk broom, and the utensils in the kitchen. The chicken with its chick riding its back surely signals the end of the famine, as Elijah prophesied.

Elijah Ascending to Heaven

Elijah, monotheism's great defender, did not suffer death but was carried to heaven. This miracle happened in the presence of Elisha, Elijah's disciple and successor, who accompanied the old seer to the River Jordan in what was his last journey. Moments before his ascension, Elijah turned to his younger companion and said, "Ask what I shall do for you, before I am taken from you." "I pray thee, let a double portion of thy spirit be upon me," the disciple replied, a wish that was granted when he saw his master enter "a chariot of fire and horses of fire" and ride to heaven in a whirlwind. In Giovanni Battista Piazzetta's canvas, *Elijah Taken Up in a Chariot of Fire*, Elisha cries out, "My father, my father" as his mentor leaves this world for the next (2 Kings 2:9–12).

Prophets were organized as a professional guild in the ancient Near East and their ranks were numerous. Elijah, who was called to this unusual occupation early in life, became the foremost seer of his day, interpreting events for kings, and eventually even anointing them. When God told him to make Elisha his successor, the latter was living on his father's large, prosperous farm. He quickly gave up his birthright, however, to minister to Elijah.

Adapting the shape of his canvas to fit the church interior for which it was commissioned, Piazzetta silhouettes Elisha against the great, fiery spectacle that marks Elijah's rise to heaven. As such, he becomes a model for all the Christian saints who saw visions. Because there was virtually an epidemic of this particular pasttime in the 16th century, theologians looked to the Old Testament for precedents. Finding this remarkable instance, they made Elisha and Elijah particular objects of veneration, along with the less illustrious beholders of heavenly sights during Piazzetta's age.

Elijah Taken Up in a Chariot of Fire
GIOVANNI BATTISTA PIAZZETTA, Italian, 1683–1754
Samuel H. Kress Collection, National Gallery of Art, Washington, D.C. Oil on canvas, 68 3/4 x 104 1/4 in.

While Elisha's reaction is predictable—what could the artist do but have him fall to his knees?—Elijah presents a more complex problem. According to the Bible, his cloak fell from his shoulders as he rose and it was taken up by Elisha. Not wanting the drapery to distract from the human dimensions of the story, particularly the prophet's amazement at what is happening to him, Piazzetta only suggests that the garment is about to slide off the old man. Instead, he devotes his attention to Elijah's face and left hand, both of which express surprise as the white steeds draw him in their wake. The horses seem to be as unfamiliar with this routine as both of the humans.

Elisha and the Children

Ordinarily Elisha was a kindly man, but the prophet also had a mean streak. This unfortunate side of his personality came to light early in the telling of his story, when he encountered a group of small boys who jeered at him and called him "Baldhead." He turned, "cursed them in the name of the Lord," and immediately "two she-bears came out of the woods and tore forty-two of the boys" apart (2 Kings 2:23–24). The savaging of these lads is the subject of *Elisha and the Children*, Barthol-omeus Breenbergh's painting of about 1635–1640.

Elisha stands in the right-central portion of the picture, his finger raised as if to say "I told you so" to the terrified youths. It is rather an empty gesture in view of the death and fear inflicted upon the boys by the giant black bears. The litter of small bodies in the lower left brings to mind the New Testament story of the Massacre of the Innocents, King Herod's slaughter of every firstborn male baby in his kingdom. What primarily distinguishes the two events is that the latter occurred at the command of an envious and cruel King, whereas God caused the slaughter of the boys who mocked Elisha. Theologians have never successfully explained the prophet's extreme reaction to the youths' insensitive but seemingly harmless taunts, but they saw in the mocking children the precursors of Christ's tormentors. Regardless of such larger meanings, Dutch parents no doubt appreciated Breenbergh's painting for the graphic lesson in good manners that it offered their children.

One of the greatest landscape painters of the generation before Rembrandt, Bartholomeus Breenbergh was among the first Dutch artists to study and paint in Italy. In fact, the desolate landscape in this work derives in part from the Roman topography that became familiar to the artist during his decade-long sojourn in the southern region. The steep hill is Italian, but the low horizon line on the right is distinctly Dutch. The same mix is evident in the architecture, as a Netherlandish church tower stands beside the ruins of an Italian citadel.

Elisha and the Children
BARTHOLOMEUS BREENBERGH, Dutch, 1598/1600–1657

Richard L. Feigen & Co., New York. Oil on wood panel, 16 ¹/₈ x 20 ⁷/₈ in.

Elisha and the Shunammite Woman
GERBRANDT VAN DEN EECKHOUT, Dutch, 1621–1674

Szépmüvészeti Museum, Budapest. Oil on canvas,
42 ¹⁵/₁₆ × 60 ½ in.

Elisha and the Shunammite Woman

A rich old woman lived with her husband in the town of Shunem, just south of Nazareth. She came to know Elisha as he passed by on his travels and in time decided to build a small lodge to shelter him when he was in her vicinity. Elisha, wanting to do something kind in return, discovered the woman's regret at not having had a child and interceded with God on her behalf. Unfortunately, the boy that she gave birth to died in his youth and the old woman came to Elisha to complain of her loss. *Elisha and the Shunammite Woman* by Gerbrandt van den Eeckhout shows their meeting high on Mount Carmel, with one of the artist's famous landscapes to the left of the figures.

Draped across the rock on which the prophet sits is the wine-colored cloak that once belonged to Elijah. This mantle came to Elisha, along with Elijah's powers of prophecy, when his master ascended to heaven. Elisha served four Hebrew kings and performed a ministry of miracles and healing that lasted over 50 years. The Bible says he was bald, and Eeckhout pictures him that way, but he appears so kindly in this painting that it is hard to believe that he once cursed some children for teasing him and stood by as two she-bears mangled them!

The Shunammite woman catches hold of Elisha's feet, as his servant Gehazi steps forward to intercede. But the prophet motions his companion back, saying "Let her alone, for she is in bitter distress; and the Lord has hidden it from me, and has not told me."

Following their meeting, Elisha examined the boy, and then brought him back to life. Again, the old woman fell at the prophet's feet, but this time in thanks (2 Kings 4:8–37).

Like his teacher Rembrandt, Gerbrandt van den Eeckhout specialized in portraits, but also painted landscapes and biblical scenes. His technique—including a brushwork much more detailed than his teacher's—is shown to great effect in *Elisha and the Shunammite Woman*. The artist not only captures the signs of age on the woman's weary countenance but also the nuances of emotion on the facial expressions of the men.

Job's Tribulations

The Book of Job is the "Greek tragedy" of the Old Testament. In it, one finds the poetic yet perplexing story of Job, the wealthiest and most righteous man of his time who fell victim to a contest between God and Satan. Believing in Job's steadfastness, the Lord wagered that the man would not lose faith even if everything that he held dear were taken from him. Satan rose to the challenge. Not only did he destroy Job's flocks of sheep, cattle, and camels, flatten his house, and cause the death of his sons and his servants, he also covered the poor man's body with painful sores. "Curse God and die" was Job's wife's advice, but the righteous man did not lose faith. Eventually, the Lord, having won his bet with Satan, returned everything to Job twofold.

The American artist James Daugherty completed his *Job* in 1946. In it he shows his protagonist doubled over in pain and confusion; a jagged flash of lightning above him symbolizes his misfortunes. Attempting to comfort him are his friends: Eliphaz, on the left, Bildad, in the middle, and Zophar, on the right. The artist's sparse use of black, gray, and white creates an atmosphere of hopeless gloom: Job is at his lowest point. Still, the strength of his faith is suggested in the muscular forms of his shoulders, arms, and legs.

The monumentality of the four figures and the way they dominate the picture plane is reminiscent of the style that was prevalent in America during the New Deal, when Federal agencies engaged artists to create murals for the lobbies of libraries, schools, and government office buildings. This work, however, was not intended as a mural but rather as an illustration for a ten-volume publication of the Bible that was never realized. *Job* would have been the frontispiece for the volume devoted to the poetic books of the Bible: Job, Psalms, Proverbs, Ecclesiastes, and the Song of Solomon.

Job

JAMES DAUGHERTY, American, 1889–1974

Salander-O'Reilly Galleries, Inc., New York. Gouache and charcoal on paper, 20 x 13 in.

The Prophet Isaiah

Isaiah was active as a prophet from about 745 to 695 B.C., a time when the entire state of Israel, except for the city of Jerusalem, was ravaged by the Assyrians. He was the author of the longest prophetic book in the Old Testament, the manuscript of which represents the oldest extant biblical writing. He was quoted more frequently in the New Testament than any other Old Testament figure. And, finally, the early 17th-century English translation of the Book of Isaiah in the Authorized (King James) Version of the Bible, whose most inspiring passages were memorialized in Handel's oratorio Messiah, ranks in eloquence with the works of Shakespeare and Milton.

Perugino's *The Prophet Isaiah* shows the sage seated in profile, and there is something regal in the figure. Perhaps the artist knew that, according to rabbinic tradition, Isaiah was the nephew of Amaziah, King of Judah. He sits on the edge of a boulder with the placement of his hands and feet giving a sense of vital animation to his body. A white scroll swirls around him, and he seems to be spontaneously chanting its inscription. The words are not his but part of the traditional liturgy. In Latin they read *"Elevata est magnificentia tua super caelos, Dominus,"* which translated means "Let your splendor rise above the heavens, O Lord." Acting as a frame within the painting's actual carved and gilded frame, the scroll seems to hold the composition in place. The format of the painting is round, as though the artist had been inspired by an ancient Roman coin. Such paintings (called *tondo*, from the Italian word for round) present a unique problem for an artist, requiring him to find a way of establishing equilibrium within the picture so that the subject does not look as if it is about to whirl away out of the painting. Perugino's solution to this problem was to place the prophet's left foot ahead of the rest of his body where it acts like a brake.

As brilliantly colored as stained glass, this *tondo* was once part of an altarpiece that featured another *tondo*, of Jeremiah, to the right. Between them was a painting of the Ascension of Jesus. Perugino, who taught the famous Raphael how to idealize physical types, was responsible for a number of frescoed cycles. He worked in the Sistine Chapel in 1481, after which he was in great demand, especially as a painter of altarpieces. Although he was apparently not a spiritual man, his art represented the summit of religious art to his contemporaries, and it enjoyed a popular resurgence in the 19th century.

The Prophet Isaiah

PIETRO PERUGINO, Italian, 1445-1523

Musée des Beaux-Arts, Nantes, France. Oil on wood panel, 51 in. diameter

The Lamentations of Jeremiah

For 40 years, the prophet Jeremiah lived with the awful knowledge of Jerusalem's impending destruction. Attempting to avert this tragedy, he sought out five successive kings of Judah, telling each in turn what could be done to save the city. But each monarch failed to heed his advice, even when his warnings grew into diatribes. Early in his career as a prophet he had complained to God that he had become "a laughingstock." "Everyone mocks me," he said, "For whenever I speak, I cry out, I shout 'Violence and destruction!'" (Jeremiah 20:7–8). Nevertheless, he divined that Jerusalem would be destroyed because of its apostasy. He saw Nebuchadnezzar I, ruler of the new Babylonian Empire, as God's instrument in chastising Judah. As the fateful last days of Jerusalem approached, he alone knew the details of what would follow, so he was accused of being an agent of the enemy, Babylonia, and thrown into a deep pit of mud. The end that he predicted came in 586 B.C., when Nebuchadnezzar leveled the city and carried off what was left of the population to Babylonia.

In *The Prophet Jeremiah Lamenting the Destruction of Jerusalem*, Rembrandt shows the discouraged old seer at the moment when his dire prophecy is coming true. Looking more tired than saddened, he rests himself against a pillar while Jerusalem burns in the background. He lived on in the rubble of Jerusalem for ten more years, but his life ended in Egypt, to which he was eventually forced to flee. He didn't survive to see the realization of his other prediction, that Judah would rise to become strong again some 70 years after Jerusalem's fall.

Rembrandt has created such a brilliant white light along the left edge of the figure of Jeremiah—so much brighter than the burning city—that the prophet appears to be enveloped in a heavenly vision. It is not clear where he is sitting or why the rich vessels are at his elbow. He himself had

no money and no family. Rembrandt may be presenting the glint of gold to symbolize the transience of wealth.   In 1630, when Rembrandt painted this disturbing yet rich portrait of desolation, he was 24 years old and living in Leiden, the city of his birth. Up to this point in his career, he had primarily painted portraits of his relatives, and probing explorations of his own face, the latter being a subject that would call to him throughout his

career. Sometimes he used costumes and accessories to transform his sitters into biblical figures. The model for Jeremiah was most likely his father, Harmen Gerritszoon van Rijn, a successful miller. With this introspective experience behind him, Rembrandt moved permanently to Amsterdam during the winter of 1631/32 and quickly rose to fame.

The Prophet Jeremiah Lamenting the Destruction of Jerusalem (Rembrandt's Father)

REMBRANDT VAN RIJN, Dutch 1606–1669

Rijksmuseum, Amsterdam. Oil on wood panel, 22 3/8 x 17 15/16 in.

The Vision of Ezekiel

Ezekiel was probably one of the Jerusalemites who witnessed the destruction of his city at the hands of the Babylonians in 586 B.C. A contemporary of Jeremiah, he had served as a priest in the city, but personal illness had prevented him from doing much to avert Jerusalem's destruction. When he did sermonize, he found as much to inveigh against as Jeremiah, but he was less abrasive, took his failures less personally, and was more visionary. Carried off to the enemy's homeland after Jerusalem's fall, he was lodging along the Chebar, a canal running off of the Euphrates River, when he was called to be a prophet.

It is the very first recorded vision of this extraordinary seer—the one that moved him to take up his new profession—that inspired Raphael's *The Vision of Ezekiel*. As described in the first chapter of the Book of Ezekiel, the prophet saw four creatures, each of which had four wings and four faces. One face was human; one was that of an eagle; the third was that of a lion; and the last that of an ox. As he watched, they ascended to the heavens, where they were transformed into the "glory of the Lord." These creatures were all ancient symbols: the eagle had been used by the Assyrians and others as a symbol of speed, omnipresence, and power over the heavens; the lion, recognized as the ruler of the animal kingdom, had appeared in prehistoric Mediterranean carvings as a symbol of might; the ox had long been worshipped by the Assyrians, a symbol of sustained strength; and the human face, of course, symbolized intellect.

Instead of consulting the Old Testament text for his imagery, Raphael, the great Renaissance artist, relied on Christian tradition. With an almost casual disregard for accuracy, he conjured up the vision of the New Testament mystic St. John, who also saw four winged creatures—a human being, an eagle, a lion, and an ox—which were interpreted to represent the Gospel writers, Matthew, Mark, Luke, and John. The principal difference between the two visions was that in Ezekiel's vision each creature had four faces; in John's, each

The Vision of Ezekiel
RAPHAEL, Italian, 1483–1520
Palazzo Pitti, Florence. Oil on wood panel, 16 x 12 in.

creature was a different species but with just one face.

Christian apologists had frequently cited Ezekiel's writings to support church decisions. Because he foretold the resettlement of Jerusalem, for example, and even provided plans for the rebuilding and refurnishing of the Temple, his name was invoked during the Middle Ages to justify the Crusades which set out to rescue Jerusalem from Moslem rule. While organizing the last of these endeavors in 1463, Pope Pius II even issued a document with the name of Ezekiel at its head. This tradition of using Old Testament figures to justify Christian ambitions led Raphael to his "misreading" of the prophet's vision.

Raphael is best known for his many renditions of the Madonna and Child, a sub

ject that he explored in a personal and highly original fashion. Unfortunately the intervening centuries have seen these works become bastardized by reproductions and inferior copies. He also painted huge, heroic frescoes in the Vatican. It is in the spirit of these monumental works that this small painting was conceived (it is only 16 inches by 12 inches). While far removed from the actual imagery of the prophet, in its statements about glory, might, and optimism *The Vision of Ezekiel* comes close to the ancient seer's spirit.

The Writing on the Wall

Belshazzar, the King of Babylonia, gave a feast for 1,000 of his lords. During the festivities he produced a set of bright golden vessels which had been ransacked from the temple in Jerusalem and brought to Babylon by Nebuchadnezzar three generations earlier. While the merry company drank wine from the vessels—a great sacrilege—and praised the gods of gold, silver, brass, iron, wood, and stone, a hand appeared and wrote a message on the plaster wall of the palace banquet hall. Terrified, the monarch asked his wise men to interpret the words, but they could not decipher them. Then at the Queen's suggestion Belshazzar summoned Daniel, a Jew known for his breadth of knowledge and the ability to interpret dreams. "God has numbered the days of your kingdom," Daniel reported, after examining the inscription. "You have been weighed in the balance and found wanting . . . your kingdom is divided and given to the Medes and Persians" (Daniel 5:2–28). According to the biblical account, Belshazzar died that very night (Daniel 5:30).

Rembrandt has frozen the moment at which Belshazzar sees the disembodied hand tracing the words on the wall. Gripped with fear, the foolish monarch knocks over one of the sacred vessels on the table. The artist leaves no questions about the status of his protagonist, whose turban has a small crown attached to it, a diamond set among its folds, and an emblem of rank dangling from it. The jewel-encrusted, fur-trimmed cape of this potentate is weighted in gold and boasts at its clasp a sunburst insignia, a symbol of kingship. Pearls and jewels sweep in a great chain towards his portly belly.

Inspiration for this work may have come from one of Rembrandt's neighbors in Amsterdam, Manasseh ben Israel, a famous rabbi and scholar, who owned one of the most important Hebrew printing houses in Europe. Rembrandt even illustrated one of his books, on Nebuchadnezzar, who was probably Belshazzar's grandfather. The artist was aware of Manasseh's interest in the inscription that magically appeared to Belshazzar on the plaster wall of the palace. The rabbi's scholarly treatise on the subject, published in Latin in 1639, argued that the King's wise men could not read the message because it was written from top to bottom rather than right to left in the traditional Hebrew manner. The words were "MENE, MENE, TEKEL, U-PHARSIN," which roughly means "Numbers, Numbers, Scales, Persians." Daniel deciphered them to mean that Belshazzar's days were numbered and his kingdom would fall to the Persians.

Rembrandt painted *Belshazzar Sees the Writing on the Wall* shortly after his arrival in Amsterdam, where he quickly achieved enormous success. Exhilarated at having money for the first time in his life, he established himself as a conspicuous spender, and flamboyant works like Belshazzar were a natural expression of his new-found status. They also reflected his profound appreciation for the art of Peter Paul Rubens. As Rembrandt learned of life's disappointments through painful personal experience, he began to concentrate more and more on the inner spirituality of his subjects.

Belshazzar Sees the Writing on the Wall
REMBRANDT VAN RIJN, Dutch, 1606–1669
The National Gallery, London. Oil on canvas, 66 x 82 3/8 in.

After the story of Adam and Eve, there is probably no Old Testament tale more familiar to children than that of Daniel in the lions' den. The story has the quality of folklore about it, and Daniel seems more a hero than the visionary and interpreter of dreams that he becomes in the Old Testament book bearing his name. Daniel was one of the noble young Jews taken to Babylon by Nebuchadnezzar in around 605 B.C. Under King Belshazzar, he rose to become viceroy of the kingdom, with status second only to that of the Queen. That he rose to such a height without ever compromising his religious beliefs made the feat even more remarkable.

When Darius succeeded Belshazzar on the throne, Daniel's responsibilities grew even greater. Jealous of the Jew's position, the monarch's other advisers encouraged him to issue an edict mandating "that whoever makes petition to any god or man for

thirty days (except to the king) shall be cast into the den of lions." Despite the ruling, Daniel continued to pray to his own god three times a day, and when this was reported to him, a very reluctant Darius had no choice but to pronounce the mandated punishment. As Daniel was taken away to the lions, Darius said to him, "May your God, whom you serve continually, deliver you!" Hoping for Daniel's salvation, the monarch fasted, refused entertainment, and spent a sleepless night. When he went to the den in the morning, he saw his viceroy alive and that "no kind of hurt was found upon him, because he had trusted in his God." Darius then had Daniel's enemies and their families thrown to the beasts. "Before they reached the bottom of the den," reported the Scriptures, "the lions overpowered them and broke all their bones in pieces." Thereafter a new proclamation was issued, this one acknowledging Daniel's deity as "the living God" (Daniel 6:7–27).

At over 7 feet in width, *Daniel in the Lions' Den* is one of Peter Paul Ruben's most powerful statements. Bones in the foreground identify the cavern as a place of execution. While the strength and great teeth of the lions are apparent, the beasts only yawn, cavort, and rest. Praying fervently, the defenseless Daniel sits on a cloak of bright red, the color that usually marks the martyr in art. Rubens seldom told a story in such a direct way, and with so few visual elements. As a great lover of the supernatural, he must have found it difficult to eliminate the angel that, according to Daniel, came to shut the lions' mouths.

By 1615, when *Daniel in the Lions' Den* was painted, the 38-year-old Rubens was already considered the leading painter in northern Europe. He had had the good fortune to study and work in Italy for eight years, and to visit Madrid where he was

Daniel in the Lions' Den

HENRY OSSAWA TANNER, American, 1859–1937

Mr. and Mrs. William Preston Harrison Collection, The Los Angeles County Museum of Art. Oil on paper mounted on canvas, 41 1/8 x 49 7/8 in.

able to peruse the royal collections of art. Having assimilated the great works of the past, he set about forging his own style, one that would capture the spirit of his era's mercantile success and royal splendor. His vigorously muscular, splendidly optimistic, and richly colorful works influenced painters for the next 300 years and came to epitomize for most people the prevailing style of 17th-century art, music, and architecture known as Baroque.

In Henry Ossawa Tanner's *Daniel in the Lions' Den*, the African-American artist of the late 19th century shows his lions as calm as their reluctant guest. The only drama in the work comes from the artist's use of lighting, with a sharp rectangle of illumination falling from an unseen window onto Daniel's helpless hands and the face of a

curious lion. The viceroy's face is in deep shadow, as are the other great yet gentle cats.

Tanner was raised in a religious household, for his father was a bishop. Early in life he painted animals, and in this work he was able to combine his love of God's creatures with his spiritual roots. Created in Paris, where Tanner spent much of his adult life, *Daniel in the Lions' Den* helped establish the artist's reputation as a leading painter of biblical subjects. Indeed it is a daring work for its reliance on light and shadow to create an inspirational mood. While Rubens emphasized an ecstatic quality in his hero, Tanner dwells on his inner faith.

Daniel in the Lions' Den
PETER PAUL RUBENS, Flemish, 1577–1640

Ailsa Mellon Bruce Fund, National Gallery of Art, Washington, D.C. Oil on canvas, 88 ¼ x 130 ⅛ in.

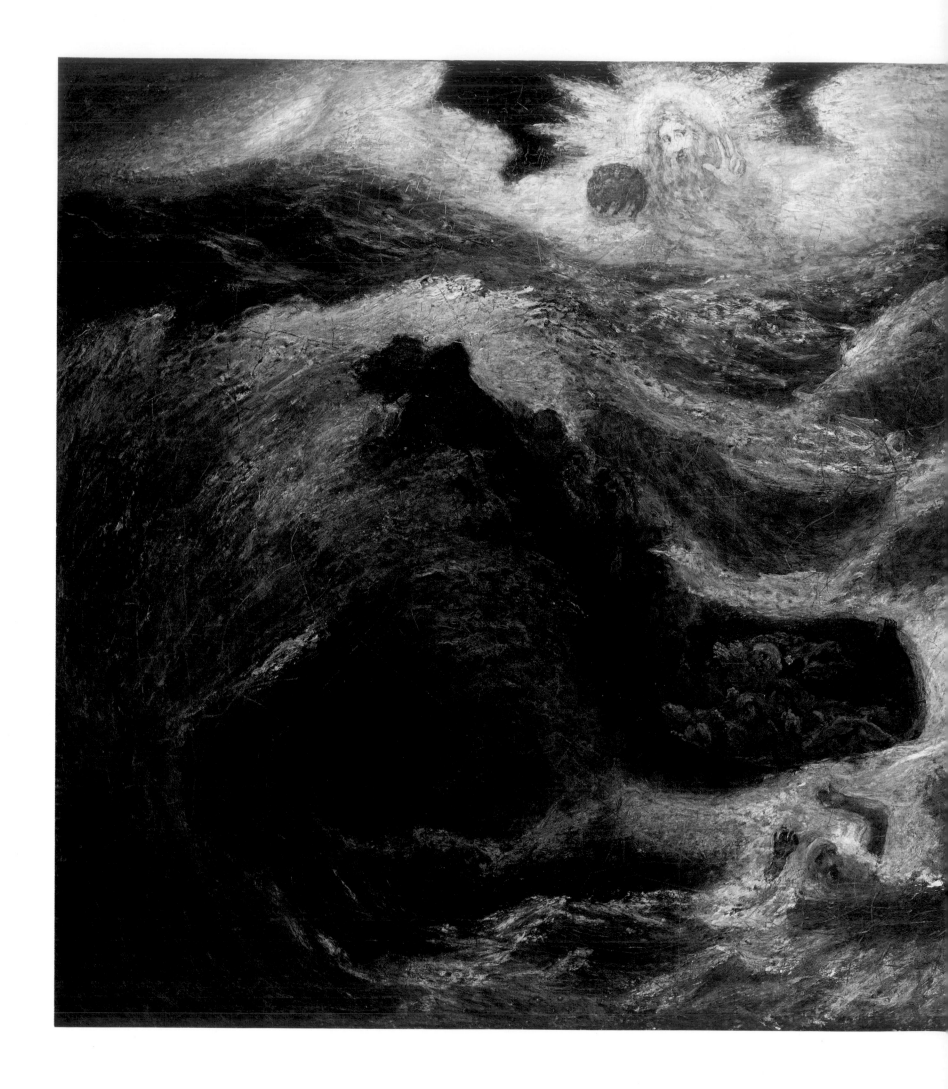

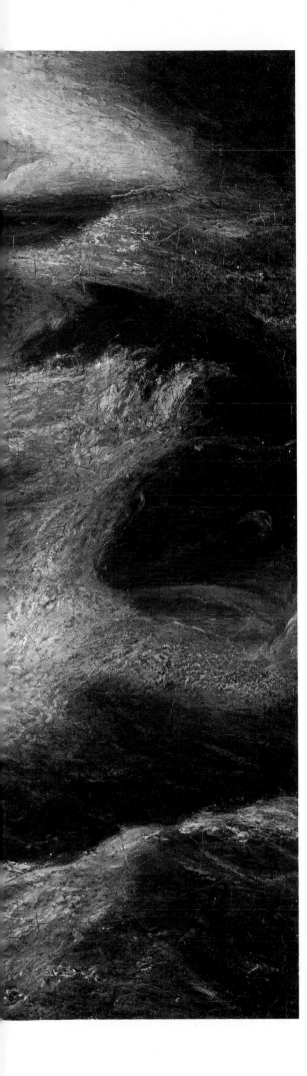

The Book of Jonah—probably the first truly memorable short story in the history of literature—related the tale of the biblical prophet who sought to evade the will of the Lord.

God wanted Jonah to go as his emissary to Nineveh, the great capital of the Assyrian Empire, and proclaim to its citizens that unless they ceased their wicked ways the whole city would be destroyed. Instead, Jonah took a boat going in the opposite direction. When the Lord caught up with him at sea, he raised a storm that tossed the fragile vessel without mercy. Jonah informed his superstitious shipmates that he was unwittingly responsible for the tumult and offered to be thrown overboard, but, not wanting to have innocent blood on their hands, the sailors rejected his offer and rowed harder. But the ship began to sink. The crew realized that they were no match for the turbulent seas and tossed their passenger into the deep. Abruptly the storm ended. As for Jonah, he was swallowed by "a great fish." After resting in the creature's belly for three days and three nights, the reluctant prophet repented, whereupon God quickly had the leviathan regurgitate him onto dry land. When asked again to go to Nineveh, he took the fastest road to that city of sin where his dire warnings caused everyone, even their King, to don sackcloth and repent (Jonah 1, 2, and 3).

Albert Pinkham Ryder, a mystic who lived in New York City, paints *Jonah* with not one whale but two, for the ship bearing the hapless prophet is also shaped like a leviathan. Perhaps Ryder thought that the sailors hovering in their vessel during the storm were converted like their passenger by this episode. The whale whose stomach was home to Jonah approaches the water-tossed seer from the upper right of the painting. Above the boat, the horizon is ablaze with the image of God winged by clouds. In giving a physical presence to the Almighty, Ryder manages to avoid reducing him to the mundane. Indeed, the Lord presides over the turbulent waves of gold and black like the Creator of the Heavens and the Earth.

Ryder was born in the fishing port of New Bedford, Massachusetts—the whaling capital of the world at the time—so he knew boats and the sea. He twice went to Europe, primarily for the voyage across the Atlantic, although he had gone to the continent on two earlier occasions to study. The art of the past, however, made little impression on him. Mainly self-taught, he relied on his own inner vision and on imaginative works of literature for inspiration. His paintings have been compared to those of Rembrandt, primarily because of their golden tonalities amid powerful passages of black, and because of their spiritual qualities. Perhaps better comparisons are to the American literary geniuses Edgar Allan Poe and Herman Melville, who were his elder contemporaries. Poe, coincidentally, was born in Massachusetts, and Melville, once a sailor, wrote *Moby Dick* while residing on a farm in the Bay State.

Jonah

ALBERT PINKHAM RYDER, American, 1847–1917

Gift of John Gellatly, National Museum of American Art, Smithsonian Institution, Washington, D.C. Oil on canvas mounted on fiberboard, 27 1/4 x 34 3/8 in.

FOLLOWING PAGES

ELSHEIMER (follower of): *Tobias and the Angel* (detail)

The Apocrypha

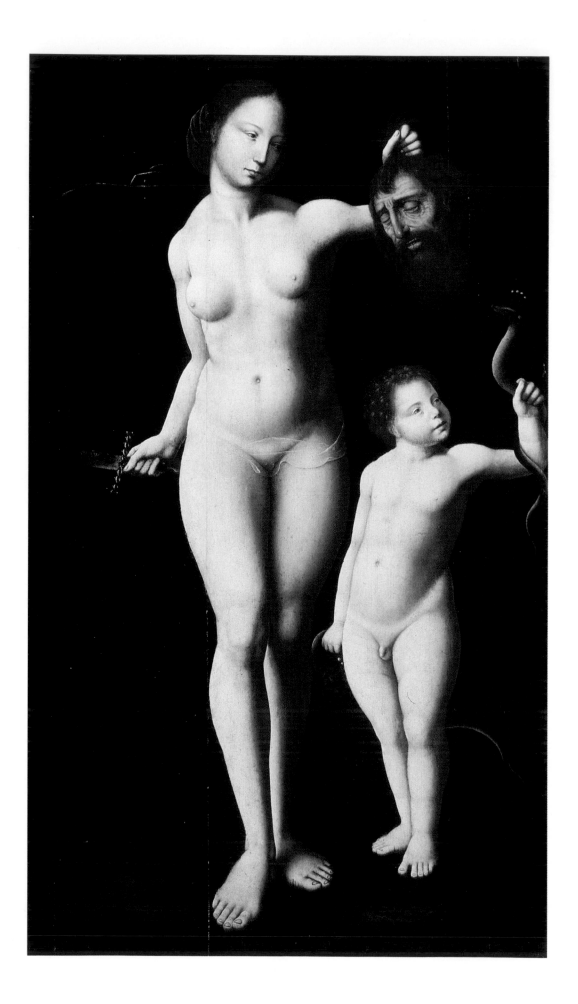

The Apocrypha, 14 books written in Hebrew or Aramaic between 200 B.C. and 100 A.D., form an integral part of the Roman Catholic Bible, and were included in the Protestant Scriptures until the 17th century. While the Puritans dropped them because they had never been part of the Hebrew Bible, artists have always valued the Apocrypha for the important lessons its stories offer. Thus, the Story of Susanna. the Book of Tobit, and the Book of Judith have inspired as many works of art over the centuries as most of the other canonical books of the Old Testament.

The Book of Judith pits a beautiful, rich, and pious widow against the powerful Assyrian general Holofernes. Nation after nation had capitulated to Holofernes' mighty army, becoming vassals to his King Nebuchadnezzar. Then he began his march on the Jews. Judith (from the Hebrew for "Jewish woman") took matters into her own hands. With her maid, she went to Holofernes, shamelessly flattered him, and convinced him that she was a refugee from the Jews. He in turn gave her his protection. After she spent three days as his guest, Holofernes invited her to dinner, hoping to seduce her. Instead, when he was "drenched with wine," she cut off his head with his own scimitar. Her maid put the grisly trophy in a bag normally reserved for kosher food, and off they went, leaving the camp guards to think that they were engaged in their usual nightly prayers. The next morning, finding their dead commander-in-chief, the Assyrians panicked and fled.

In *Judith with the Head of Holofernes*, Cristofano Allori models his heroine after his mistress, while the Assyrian general is a self-portrait. In making Judith a beautifully dressed femme fatale, he faithfully adheres to the literary text, for the Apocrypha repeatedly mentioned her stunning beauty

Judith and the Infant Hercules
MASTER OF THE MANSI MAGDALEN, Italian, active ca. 1525
The National Gallery, London. Oil on wood panel, 35 1/4 x 20 3/4 in.

and the finery that she wore to the general's tent. The maid, though almost hidden behind Judith, becomes a highly important figure in this painting, for in the awe and adoration that she shows her brave mistress she foreshadows the reaction of the Jews when they learn of Judith's deed.

In his day, Allori was the leading painter of Florence, and his *Judith with the Head of Holofernes* symbolizes a critical change in the history of his proud, small city-state. As a dukedom, Florence no longer embraced the symbol of its republican years, the young David, slayer of Goliath. In Allori's lifetime, the most memorable member of the Medicis, the dynasty that had given the city its rulers since the mid-15th century, was Catherine. Though dead by the time of this painting's execution, the woman who became Queen of France and the mother of three kings was wistfully remembered. She summed up all the qualities desired in a ruler. So too did Judith. Thus, the Jewish heroine quietly displaced David as the new symbol of Florence's patriotic aspirations, and this picture was hung on the walls of the ducal palace to remind its occupants to marry well.

An anonymous artist from Flanders turned to antiquity rather than the Apocrypha to inspire his depiction of *Judith and the Infant Hercules*. Although the Jewess bathed daily as part of her religious ritual, she never appeared naked before Holofernes. That the artist shows her unclothed might indicate an awareness of the origins of the Judith saga in Greek mythology, where there is a similar tale featuring the virgin goddess Athena. Although the Goddess of War was ordinarily shown in armor, the artist in this case thinks that the best way to dress his heroine (Judith/Athena) for a seduction scene is to undress her. She is accompanied by the infant Hercules, who learned bravery at her side.

Judith with the Head of Holofernes
CRISTOFANO ALLORI, Italian, 1577–1621
Palazzo Pitti, Florence. Oil on canvas, 35 1/4 x 20 3/4 in.

Susanna and the Elders

The Book of Susanna, probably written during the 1st century B.C., has never been accepted as part of the authentic, or divinely inspired, canon of the Bible, but because it featured Daniel as a judge it has been appended to the Book of Daniel in some versions of the Holy Scriptures, most notably those used in Roman Catholicism. Ranked by some as one of the finest short stories in world literature, it told the tale of a young and beautiful woman who triumphed over lust and lies.

Susanna and her husband were Jewish exiles in Babylonia. One day, while she was bathing, two prominent men of her city spied on her. Excited by her beauty, they threatened to ruin her reputation if she did not give in to their lustful desires. She was steadfast in her refusal, so they publicly accused her of committing adultery with a young man, and she was condemned to death. Daniel, however, interceded in the matter, questioning each of her accusers in private. When his investigation revealed significant contradictions in their stories, he ruled in favor of the beautiful heroine, condemning her accusers to death instead.

Jacob Jordaens, a devoutly religious man, introduced an uncharacteristic note of hilarity into his depiction of *Susanna and the Two Elders* by caricaturing the principals involved. The "beauty," overweight and lacking in grace, has the body of a middle-aged man, one that is overly large for her delicate head. By the coy half-smile on her face, she seems to enjoy the attention of the two leering fools. One of them clumsily throws a leg across the wall that separates him and his fellow letch from the object of their desire. but he clearly does not have the strength to carry the rest of

his body over the enclosure. If he were to succeed in his overly ambitious acrobatics, he would end up in the bath with Susanna. She is surrounded by a display of vulgarly overwrought accessories, and only the chaste white linen draped across her tub suggests purity. Her lapdog's shrill bark might be the only evidence of conscience in this wickedly fanciful morality painting by one of the greatest religious artists of northern Europe. Jordaens, by the way, was 60 years of age when he painted this work, so he may have sympathized with the physical limitations of the elders.

Thomas Hart Benton, the "old salt" of 20th-century American Scene painters—as the regionalist artists of the 1920s and 1930s were known—understood the universality of this story. His Susanna is a modern woman skinny-dipping in a country stream. Her bright red high-heeled shoes, matched by the color of her painted fingernails, indicate her city origins. Just as Susanna of old was a captive in Babylonia, so this modern incarnation is an exile—or at least out of her element—in this bucolic setting. Open-toed shoes and enameled fingertips were frowned upon in rural America, so the word of the two gentlemen who claimed that "she invited what she deserved" would no doubt have been accepted by their neighbors. Benton's elders are local farm gentry, one of whom has parked his Model T next to the horse and wagon of the other. Both vehicles are close to the white painted church that represents not their faith but their hypocrisy.

Benton executed numerous studies of the foliage in this painting, referring to samples from nature that he brought into his studio. He also used a model for Susanna whose stiffness at holding such a precarious pose comes through in the painting. He painstakingly built up layers of translucent oil glazes over an egg tempera foundation to achieve the purity of flesh tones that make this such a startling work of art. (Egg tempera was the favored medium of artists of the late Middle Ages and early Renaissance.) Surely, he must have considered this, one of his few excursions into biblical subject matter, a major artistic statement.

Susanna and the Elders
THOMAS HART BENTON, American, 1889–1975
The Fine Arts Museum of San Francisco, San Francisco. Egg tempera on canvas mounted on panel, 60 x 42 in.

While Benton's nature setting and contemporary twist to the story make his *Susanna and the Elders* an unusually provocative painting, it should be noted that Jordaens used contemporary accessories in his work as well, and modeled his elders after the buffoons of the drama of his day. Thus both artists treated the story as a morality lesson for their peers rather than as a tale from history.

DETAIL
Susanna and the Two Elders

FOLLOWING PAGES
Susanna and the Two Elders
JACOB JORDAENS, Flemish, 1593–1678
Statens Museum for Kunst, Copenhagen. Oil on canvas, 59 7/8 x 79 1/16 in.

Tobias and the Angel

One of the most popular of the apocryphal texts, the Book of Tobit, told the story of a Jew of the Diaspora named Tobit and his son Tobias. Although he was blinded, reduced to poverty, and taken to the pagan country of Nineveh after the destruction of the Northern Kingdom of Israel in the 8th century, B.C., the once-wealthy Tobit continued to follow the teachings of his youth, practicing charity every day of his life. He was regularly punished for his acts, and his wife and friends called him a fool for continuing them.

Tobit's one earthly comfort was Tobias, his son. In *Tobias and the Angel*, Adam Elsheimer shows the lad on a mission to fetch the family's fortune left in the hands of a friend by Tobit before the fall of the Hebrew kingdom. Tobias' companion is the Archangel Raphael. Although he was disguised as a family member named Azarias (meaning "God helps") in the literary account, artists delighted in showing him with wings.

In this beautifully rendered painting, young Tobias drags behind him the fish that almost ate him when he went to the river's edge to wash. Without losing stride, but slowed by the weight of his finned cargo, he listens as the angel explains that the fish has special powers—not only will its entrails dispel demons, they will also restore sight. As it happened, these powers came in handy, for the woman that Raphael had chosen to be Tobias' wife was plagued by a demon-lover so jealous that he had killed seven men for attempting to take her in marriage. The entrails sent the demon packing, and Tobias won his bride. Upon his return home, he used the fish's insides again, this time to restore his father's sight.

Elsheimer painted only twenty-four pic

tures in his short life, two of which were devoted to the story of Tobias and the angel. The most popular of the two was lost, but it is known through fine copies, such as this one. Elsheimer had an enormous influence on several generations of artists who strived to learn his meticulous style by replicating his works. These copies also attest to the popularity of the story of Tobit and his son, particularly in the early 17th century when individual piety was on the rise.

Tobias and the Angel

Mid-17th century Flemish copy after ADAM ELSHEIMER, German, 1578–1610

The National Gallery of Art, London. Oil on copper, 7 5/8 x 10 7/8 in.

The Peaceable Kingdom
EDWARD HICKS, American, 1780–1849
Worcester Art Museum, Massachusetts. Oil on canvas,
17 ½ x 23 ¹¹/₁₆ in

The Peaceable Kingdom

Malachi, the last of the Old Testament prophets, wearily examined the sins of his people and asked them, "Have we not all one father? Has not one God created us? Why then are we faithless to one another?" (Malachi 2:10). He looked toward a day when "the sun of righteousness shall rise, with healing in its wings" and the children of Israel "shall go forth leaping like calves from the stall" (Malachi 4:2).

The Old Testament is a history of God's chosen people and their struggle to keep his laws. Its heroes are the Malichis who correct them, set them on the high path, and make them right with God. It is also a book of hope, one that looks for the sun to shine on a day when all men and women will share the innocence and joy of Malachi's leaping calves. This book ends with an image that comes close to Malachi's vision. *The Peaceable Kingdom* by Edward Hicks is inspired by the poetic prophecy of Isaiah: "The wolf shall dwell with the lamb, and the leopard shall lie down with the kid, and the calf and the lion and the fatling together, and a little child shall lead them" (Isaiah 11:6). Like the prophets of the Old Testament, Hicks based his utopian dream on the history of his own sect, the Quakers. A preacher of the sect himself, he depicts William Penn, the founder of the movement in America, in the left background, confirming a treaty of peace with the Indians.

Edward Hicks was best known in his own day as a preacher. His paintings were primarily executed as gifts for friends. So deeply did he believe in the coming of a Peaceable Kingdom and so great was his desire to share that vision with his loved ones that he made more than a hundred versions of this painting between 1820 and 1849. His simple sermon is as powerful in its message as the miracles of Moses, the visions of Isaiah, or the dreams of Malachi, and it is as enduring for art lovers and lovers of peace as the words it illustrates.

About the Artists

Cristofano Allori, Italian, 1577–1621 Born into an important family of artists, Allori became the most famous painter of his day in the city of Florence. His use of rich color and dramatic subject matter paved the way for the style of the Baroque. His most memorable painting is illustrated in this book.

Washington Allston, American, 1779–1843 The son of a wealthy South Carolina family, Allston studied art in England with Benjamin West and Henry Fuseli. Between 1813 and 1817, he produced a series of large and impressive religious paintings that mark him as one of the most important biblical painters in the romantic tradition. He lived abroad on and off until 1818, when he returned permanently to the United States to be hailed as the country's finest living artist.

Andrea del Castagno, Italian, 1417/19–1457 Andrea del Castagno was in the vanguard of the celebrated artists of Florence during the heady years when the Italian Renaissance style was coming into vogue. Although he was not an innovator himself, he embodied the realism of Donatello and the monumentality of Masaccio, creating intensely energetic works, most of which dealt with Biblical subjects.

Bacchiacca (Francesco Urbertini Verdi), Italian, 1494–1557 Bacchiacca, one of the students of Pietro Perugino, centered his career in his native city, Florence. He is known for his small figures in cityscapes. Their poses and costumes are often bizarre, lending a highly decorative quality to his paintings

Hans Baldung Grien, German, 1484/5–1545 One of the most prolific and versatile artists of his day, Hans Baldung, surnamed Grien for the frequent use of green in his work, lived and worked primarily in Strasbourg. He designed stained glass and tapestries, and produced a large body of book illustrations and other graphic works as well as paintings. His best known work is the altarpiece for the cathedral in Freiburg im Breisgau. He had a strong taste for the gruesome and the erotic in subject matter.

Thomas Hart Benton, American, 1889–1975 Born in Missouri, Benton began his career as a newspaper cartoonist. After a number of years in Paris, he led the movement to create a distinctly

BOSCH: *The Garden of Paradise*

American style of painting that would reflect the thoughts and aspirations of the masses. Called the Regionalist Group, or American Scene painters, he and his colleagues dominated American art from the 1920s until just after World War II.

Biagio di Antonio, Italian, active 1476–1504 During his short life, Biagio di Antonio painted a number of charming *cassone* panels, probably as an assistant in the workshop of one of the more famous Florentine artists. His works demonstrate a mastery of Renaissance principals, but at the same time are old-fashioned in their decorative qualities.

Bonifazio de' Pitati, Italian, 1487–1553 Bonifazio de' Pitati was strongly influenced by his contemporaries and compatriots Giorgione and Titian. He ran a large workshop in Venice and seems to have won the patronage of that city's intellectuals.

Hieronymus Bosch, Dutch, ca. 1450–1516 Few artists in history have had as fertile and inventive an imagination as had Hieronymus Bosch. In spite of his unconventional and bizarre imagery, his fantasies were respected during his own lifetime and he had a successful career. Seventeenth-century critics, however, saw his paintings as heretical. Though only about 40 works by him are extant, prints of his designs were widely circulated during his own lifetime and led to many imitations.

Cecco Bravo (Francesco Montelatici), Italian, 1601–1661 One of the leading artists of Florence, Cecco Bravo left Medici patronage to serve the court at Innsbruck in Austria.

Jan de Bray, Dutch, 1627–1691 Primarily a portrait painter, de Bray spent his entire career in his hometown of Haarlem. He was influenced by his illustrious contemporary compatriate Frans Hals, but he developed a smoother style that appealed to more conservative tastes. His father was an esteemed architect and painter.

Bartholomeus Breenbergh, Dutch, 1598/1600–1657 After spending a decade painting in Italy, Bartholomeus Breenbergh helped create a taste for Italianate subjects in Holland. The countryside around Rome, with ancient ruins, frequently appears in his biblical and mythological paintings. Late in his life, he lessened the focus on landscape in his paintings, turning to the figure as primary subject matter.

Ford Madox Brown, English, 1821–1893 Brown spent his early years in continental Europe, where he was trained. Settling in England in 1845, he quickly became an influential figure. His friends included the Pre-Raphaelite artists, with whom he shared social ideals. He designed furniture and stained glass for William Morris' company, which led a movement to return to medieval models of craftsmanship. Brown spoke out against the hegemony of the Royal Academy in matters of art and pioneered the idea of one-man exhibitions.

Jan Bruegel the Elder, Flemish, 1568–1625 The son of the artist Pieter Bruegel the Elder, Jan Bruegel the Elder worked in Italy for the powerful Cardinal Federico Borromeo before settling in Antwerp at the age of 29. He continued to have rich and eminent patrons, and became a close

friend of Peter Paul Rubens, with whom he sometimes collaborated. A famous result of their joint efforts is depicted in this book. Although it shows his expertise at painting animals, he was more famous as a landscape and flower painter and earned the nickname "Velvet" because of his extraordinary ability to paint delicate textures.

Pieter Bruegel the Elder, Flemish, ca. 1525–1569 Universally regarded as one of the great inventive geniuses in Western art, Pieter Bruegel the Elder was befriended by the most important thinkers of his day. Through the use of allegory and proverbs, he faithfully recorded the suffering and misery that befell the Low Countries during the 16th century. A number of his designs were used for engravings, allowing his work wide distribution. He lived mainly in Antwerp and Brussels.

Hans Burgkmair the Elder, German, 1473–1531 Along with Albrecht Dürer, Burgkmair was responsible for turning German art from the style of the Middle Ages to the sensibilities of the Renaissance. It is assumed that he spent time south of the Alps before settling in his native Augsburg. He was employed from time to time by the Emperor Maximilian and is as famous for his woodcuts as for his portraits and biblical history paintings.

Valerio Castello, Italian, 1625–1659 Valerio Castello was well on his way to becoming the major fresco painter of his day, when he died prematurely at the age of 34. His fresh and dramatic paintings decorate many of the palaces of Genoa, where he lived and worked. He specialized in religious and historical subjects.

Marc Chagall, Russian, 1887–1985 Though active mainly in France and a member of the so-called School of Paris which opened up the art world to modernism, Chagall also had careers in Russia and America. After the Russian Revolution, he established an academy of art in his native city of Vitebsk, Belorussia, and designed sets for the newly formed Jewish Theatre in Moscow. But the element of fantasy in his work was not approved by the Soviet authorities, and he became an expatriate. His vast output includes costume and set designs, book illustrations and other graphics, and designs for large stained glass compositions and murals. Along with Georges Rouault, he ranks as the leading religious artist of the 20th century.

Cima da Conegliano (Giovanni Battista Cima), Italian, 1460(?)–1517/18(?) Cima's work represents one of the high points of the Renaissance in Venice. Calmer and more devotional than Florentine paintings of the same period, they are weighty and imbued with a feeling of inner peace. His work has been likened to that of his more famous contemporary Giovanni Bellini and to the earlier Florentine master Masaccio.

Lovis Corinth, German, 1858–1925 After studying in France, Corinth became one of the leaders of the German Impressionist school. A stroke incapacitated him in 1911, and he was forced to paint in a looser style thereafter, but his works still retained power. The voluptuousness of his religious and allegorical subjects distinguish them from his landscapes, portraits, and still lifes.

Pietro da Cortona, Italian, 1596–1669 One of the greatest architects and painters of his age, Pietro da Cortona helped define the Roman Baroque style. Famous for illusionistic ceiling paintings full of exuberant figures and clouds parting to reveal heaven to the viewer below, and for using paintings to unify carved stucco figures, his work strongly influenced the glorious style of church and palace decoration that dominated Europe for a century.

Lucas Cranach the Elder, German, 1472–1553 The court painter to three successsive Electors of Saxony, Lucas Cranach was a friend and neighbor of Martin Luther and is called "the painter of the Reformation." His many portraits of the famous Protestants of his age are among his best works. He was aided by a large studio of students and assistants who executed multiple copies of many of his paintings.

James Daugherty, American, 1889–1974 Born in Westport, Connecticut, Daugherty was an author and illustrator as well as a muralist. The WPA (Works Progress Administration) supported his career during the late years of the Great Depression. He died in Asheville, North Carolina.

Willem Drost, Dutch, active 1652–1680 Almost nothing is known of the life of Drost, but six or so extant paintings by him and a few etchings—all dating from the 1650s—indicate that he was one of the most talented followers of Rembrandt.

Albrecht Dürer, German, 1471–1528 Dürer was the most important and famous northern European artist of his day. He brought Italian Renaissance concerns about perspective, ideal beauty, proportion, and harmony to his paintings, engravings, and woodcuts, and his art remained highly influential for generations after his death. Indeed, the quality of his graphic production is still unsurpassed. A native of Nuremberg, where he worked all his life, Dürer traveled throughout northern Europe and Italy on a number of occasions, and his diary of one of these trips (in 1520/21) gives the modern reader insight into the goals and problems of this great artist.

Gerbrandt van den Eeckhout, Dutch, 1621–1674 Like many of the other students of Rembrandt, Gerbrandt van den Eeckhout used a broad touch close to that of his master in his religious works, but he developed a separate style for other subjects. His genre paintings are marked by tight, exacting brushwork. He also painted portraits of many of the prominent citizens of Amsterdam, the city where he was born.

Adam Elsheimer, German, 1578–1610 Elsheimer lived most of his short life in Rome, where he came into contact with Rubens and other artists who greatly admired the intense and

DÜRER: *Adam*

minutely precise paintings on which he worked very slowly. After Dürer, he is regarded as Germany's most important artist. Most of his paintings are on copper, which preserves the purity of color, unlike canvas and wood, on which colors change with age.

Gaudenzio Ferrari, Italian, ca. 1471/81–1546 Because he was active in remote areas of Italy, the work of Gaudenzio Ferrari is not well known. However, his work, which is highly charged with emotional content, reflects the powerful influence of such contemporaries as Leonardo da Vinci, Pordenone, and Lorenzo Lotto.

Erastus Salisbury Field, American, 1805–1900 Of all the so-called naive or primitive painters of America, none created a body of work displaying greater variety than Erastus Salisbury Field. At the start of his long career as a limner, he concentrated on portraits of family members and neighbors in

the small, rural community of Leverett, Massachusetts, where he lived most of his life. Word of mouth gave him portrait commissions in other New England towns, but the popularity of the newly invented art of photography drove him to new subject matter. From the years immediately before the Civil War until the end of his life, he painted landscapes and biblical and historical subjects.

Henry Fuseli (Johann Heinrich Füssli), Anglo-Swiss, 1741–1825 Born in Zurich, the son of a portrait painter, Fuseli became a priest and turned to painting only after he moved to England and met Sir Joshua Reynolds. He then spent eight years studying the work of Michelangelo in Italy, after which he produced the imaginative and often nightmarish paintings that form the basis of his reputation as one of the leading Romantic painters of his age.

Paul Gauguin, French, 1848–1903 At the age of 35, Gauguin gave up a successful livelihood as a stockbroker and turned his weekend avocation, painting, into a full-time career. Seeking a style not affected by the "disease of civilization," he lived for periods of time in Tahiti, where, in abject poverty, he created much of his best work. His highly personal style is rich in color and linear patterns abstracted from nature.

Baron François-Pascal-Simon Gérard, French, 1770–1837 The favorite pupil of the famous Jacques-Louis David, Gérard gained fame early in his career, and became a fashionable painter of portraits. Napoleon commissioned him to execute a mammoth work commemorating the Battle of Austerlitz, and when the monarchy was restored he quickly became chief painter to Louis XVIII, who made him a baron and heaped other honors upon him.

Giorgione (Giorgio Barbarelli, or Giorgio del Castelfranco), Italian, ca. 1478–1510 Almost nothing is known of this great artist's life, but Giorgione's work influenced Venetian painting for almost 100 years after his death in his early thirties of the plague. He softened outlines and color through the use of pervading atmospheric light, creating works that are luminous and warm. Upon his death, Titian completed at least one of his paintings.

Giovanni di Paolo, Italian, active 1420–1482 The small paintings of religious subjects by Giovanni di Paolo reflect the spirituality of Siena, where the artist was active during the years immediately following the outbreak of bubonic plague that wiped out many of the city's most famous painters. The almost whimsical figures that inhabit his often dramatically lighted, spare landscapes make his strange paintings among the most appealing and engaging of 15th-century Siena.

Guercino (Giovanni Francesco Barbieri), Italian, 1591–1666 A product of north Italian training,

Guercino went to Rome to serve Pope Gregory XV, and there he produced works in Rome that are exuberant and illusionistic. In 1642 he moved to Bologna to take over the workshop of Guido Reni, an influential artist who had recently died. Guercino remained in Bologna for the rest of his life, becoming that city's leading painter. Drawings by Guercino are among the most highly valued of all 17th-century draftsmen.

Jean-Jacques Henner, French, 1829–1905 At the outset of his career Henner won the coveted Prix de Rome with a painting of Adam and Eve mourning the body of Abel (reproduced herein). This award enabled him to spend the next six years studying the old masters in Italy. Upon his return to France, he made his reputation painting sensuous nudes, marking a rather significant departure from the portraits he had created in his youth.

Edward Hicks, American, 1780–1849 A sign and coach painter, Hicks used the flat, stylized, decorative style of his trade to produce a body of charming, moralistic paintings that are among the best known and most popular of all 19th-century American folk art. A Quaker preacher, most of his works focus on the blessings of peace and the innocence of Eden, themes that were preoccupations of his religion

Melchior de Hondecoeter, Dutch, 1636–1695 The son and grandson of artists, Melchior de Hondecoeter was a specialist in painting birds. His accurately drawn and colored barnyard fowl and exotic avians often pantomime fables such as those of Aesop. Early in his life, Hondecoeter trained to be a preacher. His paintings are full of moral lessons and were popular with farmers as well as princes. Although *Animals from Noah's Ark*, illustrated in this book, is his only overtly biblical painting, many of his works include veiled references to Holy Scripture.

William Holman Hunt, English, 1827–1910 One of the founders of a group of artists called the Pre-Raphaelite Brotherhood, Hunt and his small circle sought to bring the sincerity and simplicity of early Italian painting to the art of their day. Though critics have always thought that his influence on his own times was more important than his actual paintings, the authentic details in his works deserve respect.

Jacob Jordaens, Flemish, 1593–1678 In 1640, Jacob Jordaens became the chief painter of Antwerp following the death in 1640 of his friend and colleague, Peter Paul Rubens, who had dominated the art of his time. A Protestant by conversion late in his life, Jordaens crossed the Dutch border into the Netherlands every week so that he could worship in freedom, for his religion was banned in Flanders. The artist nevertheless served the Catholics of his city by painting numerous altarpieces for their churches. He imbued his figures with a feeling of robust energy and innocent faith.

Wassily Kandinsky, Russian, 1866–1944 Among the very first artists in history to paint purely abstract works, Kandinsky is one of the giants of the modern art movement. After studying in Munich, he held important academic posts in Russia, then moved to Germany in 1921 to take a teaching post at the newly formed Bauhaus, the first school created to teach modernism in design and the visual arts. When it was closed down by the Nazis in 1933, Kandinsky moved to France and eventually became a French citizen. His writings, including a book called *Concerning the Spiritual in Art* (1912), were as influential as his paintings in stimulating artists to think about their craft in new ways.

Charles Le Brun, French, 1619–1690 As the leading art theorist of his day and chief painter to King Louis XIV, Le Brun unified standards of taste and codified a system of orthodoxy in art favoring Classicism. His ideas dominated French art well into the 19th century. The Grand Manner associated with Louis XIV was also Le Brun's creation. He and his workshop of hundreds of assistants were responsible for the design of tapestries, furniture, sculpture, and the decor of the state's principal palaces, as well as many of the paintings that found their way into these royal domiciles.

Filippino Lippi, Italian, 1457(?)–1504 Filippino Lippi, the son of painter Fra Filippo Lippi, was a student of the famous Botticelli, and during his lifetime he achieved a reputation as great as that of his celebrated teacher. Responsible for many church frescoes in his native Florence, Lippi was one of the leading artists of the Italian Renaissance. His works are inventive, tender, and beautifully detailed.

Claude Lorrain (Claude Gelée), French, 1600–1682 The leading landscape painter of the 17th century and one of the most influential artists of all time, Claude Lorrain lived and worked in Rome, where the patronage of Pope Urban VIII helped him rise to fame. While his poetic treatment of the landscape gave it legitimacy for the first time as a subject of its own, he often added tiny figures from the Bible, ancient history, or mythology to "elevate" his work to the status of history painting.

Lucas van Leyden, Dutch, 1494–1533 Lucas van Leyden produced his first engraving at the age of 14. This work was followed by an unbroken series of engravings that spanned his entire life. A prodigious worker, he also produced woodcuts and etchings and was a master draftsman. His paintings demonstrate eloquent religious feeling. Although he had no known students or direct followers, his work later inspired Rembrandt, who was also born in Leiden.

Andrea Mantegna, Italian, 1431–1506 One of the greatest Italian Renaissance painters and engravers, Andrea Mantegna worked mainly in Mantua and Padua. Known for his bold use of perspective and extreme foreshortening of the human form, his paintings are relatively rare. Of a number of large series that he executed, only *The Triumph of Caesar* still exists (Hampton Court, London).

Master of the Mansi Magdalen, Italian, active ca. 1525 A follower of Quentin Massys (1465/6–1530), the Master of the Mansi Magdalen is thought to have been Netherlandish. From his works, it is apparent that he was familiar with the engravings of Albrecht Dürer, for his paintings reflect the ideas of the great German artist. His appelation comes from a painting of Mary Magdalen attributed to him. It is now in Berlin and named for a former owner.

Master of the Twelve Apostles, Italian, active first half of the 16th century Nothing is known of the Master of the Twelve Apostles, whose appelation comes from an altarpiece attributed to his hand.

Hans Memling, Flemish, 1433–1494 The soft, sweet religious paintings for which Memling is famous made the artist one of the richest citizens of Bruges, in his time the greatest port of northern Europe. His conservative style appealed not only to his fellow citizens but also to the rich Italian bankers who were living in his city. Knowing a good thing, he hardly changed his style during his entire career.

Michelangelo Buonarroti, Italian, 1475–1564 Michelangelo was one of the mightiest figures of the Italian Renaissance. His contributions to any one of the fields in which he excelled—poetry, architecture, painting, sculpture, and draftsmanship—could alone justify his fame. The term High Renaissance was invented to distinguish his work, and that of Raphael and Leonardo da Vinci, his contemporaries, from the work of all the masters who had gone before them.

Frans van Mieris I, Dutch, 1635–1681 Like Rembrandt and Lucas van Leyden, Frans van Mieris I was born in Leiden. He was famous for his domestic genre scenes and was father to three artists who carried on his tradition of producing paintings in a highly polished style.

Jean-François Millet, French, 1814–1875 Born

JORDAENS: *Moses Striking Water from the Rock*

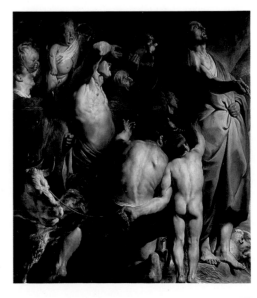

173

into a peasant family, Millet specialized in creating paintings that dignified the toilers in the fields. His social consciousness made him a hero to the later generations of Impressionists and Post-Impressionists, and his most famous work, *The Angelus*, was the most widely reproduced painting of the 19th century.

Iaes Corneliszoon Moeyart, Dutch, ca. 1592–1655 After a sojourn in Italy, Moeyaert fell under the spell of his countryman, Rembrandt. He was an important enough artist in Amsterdam to be chosen, with others, to create decorations for the triumphal entry of Maria de' Medici into that city in 1638. He also served the King of Denmark.

Gustave Moreau, French, 1826–1898 In opposition to the naturalism of the Impressionists and the Realism of the Academy, Moreau invented an individualistic and quirky style of his own. Sensuous, mystical, and highly symbolic, it was very popular even though the artist never tried to sell his work. Late in his life he became an influential teacher whose students included Henri Matisse and Georges Rouault.

Edvard Munch, Norwegian, 1863–1944 Considered his country's greatest artist, Munch treated subjects of psychological depth with extraordinary honesty and intensity. Jealousy, mental illness, and the awakening of sexual desire are recurrent themes. His wood engravings, lithographs, and etchings are as highly influential today as his paintings.

Bartolomé Esteban Murillo, Spanish, 1617–1682 Murillo was the leading painter of Seville, the city of his birth, where he helped to establish an art academy. While he is best known for his sweet Madonnas, he painted many other religious subjects, as well as portraits that are considered by some to be his finest works. He is not as highly regarded today as he was in centuries past, but his ability to tell stories in straightforward, simple terms suggests that a reevaluation of his talent may be in order.

Charles Joseph Natoire, French, 1700–1777 A rival of the famous François Boucher, Natoire won the Prix de Rome in 1725. Later, he returned to the Eternal City to direct the French Academy there. Preferring Old Testament and Classical subjects, Natoire produced a large body of work, including church decorations and tapestry designs.

Giovanni Antonio Pellegrini, Italian, 1675–1741 Pellegrini helped spread the Venetian Rococo style to Austria, England, France, Germany, and the Netherlands, countries where he decorated palaces, great houses, and public buildings. His light, airy, and colorful paintings are routine by today's standards, but at the time they brought a new level of elegance to northern Europe.

Pietro Perugino, Italian, 1445–1523 Little is known of Perugino's early life, but his reputation was established by the frescoes that he painted in the Sistine Chapel at the age of 35. Thereafter, he received a steady stream of commissions for frescoes, portraits, and primarily altarpieces. The latter are sweet and sentimental but were very popular in his day. He was the teacher of Raphael.

Giovanni Battista Piazzetta, Italian, 1683–1754 A notoriously slow painter, Piazzetta relied on book illustration to earn a living. Nonetheless, his paintings managed to appear fresh and spontaneous and were highly regarded. As the first director of the Venice Academy of Fine Arts, he influenced many young artists, teaching the dramatic and serious style of a century earlier. Late in his life, however, he adopted the new, lighter feeling of the Rococo.

Jacopo da Pontormo, Italian, 1494–1557 A student of Leonardo da Vinci, Jacopo da Pontormo was one of the primary inventors of the style known as Mannerism. He developed his peculiarly restless vision early on, and the success of his paintings turned artists away from

the symmetry and order of the Renaissance, a style that had dominated art for two generations. Except for some extraordinarily perceptive portraits, and some mythological scenes, the bulk of his work was devoted to religious subjects.

Nicolas Poussin, French, 1594–1665 Inspired by the art of antiquity, Poussin created scenes drawn from ancient and biblical history that brought him enormous fame during his lifetime. Regarded as the greatest living artist of his day, he worked primarily in Italy, where he formulated the ideas that influenced French artists for 300 years.

Sir Edward John Poynter, English, 1836–1919 Famous for his large and carefully researched historical tableaux, Poynter was one of the most popular artists of his day. Trained in Italy and France, he was a splendid draftsman and also a tireless administrator. Knighted by Queen Vicoria in 1896, he directed major museums and an art school, and was president of the Royal Academy from 1896 to 1918.

Pierre Puvis de Chavannes, French, 1824–1898 A student of Delacroix and Couture, Pierre Puvis de Chavannes was primarily inspired by classical art. His sale of a painting to the French government in 1861 brought him widespread attention. Thereafter, he was in considerable demand in Paris and elsewhere. The murals that he created in his chaste and subdued style can be found in the Hotel de Ville, the Sorbonne, and the Panthéon in Paris, and the Boston Public Library in the United States.

Raphael (Raffaello Sanzio), Italian, 1483–1520 One of the most celebrated artists of all time, Raphael created works that epitomized the harmony and balance of High Renaissance composition. Under Pope Leo X, he was responsible for major projects in the Vatican, including huge paintings in the Stanza della Segnatura. He also designed numerous churches, palaces, and mansions. His fame in the 19th century was based primarily on his numerous renditions of the Madonna and Child.

Rembrandt (Rembrandt Hermensz van Rijn), Dutch, 1606–1669 The leading portrait and biblical painter of the Netherlands, Rembrandt spent most of his career in Amsterdam, where he was a conspicuous figure, initially for his fertile talent and extravagant lifestyle, and later for his public bankruptcy, the breadth of his knowledge, and the depth of his work. As a painter of religious themes, he towers above all others for his ability to empathize with the subjects of his art.

José de Ribera, Spanish, 1591–1652 Known as "Lo Spagnoletto," José de Ribera lived most of his life in Naples, which was ruled by Spain at the time. He was famous for his ability to imbue "portraits" of saints, patriarchs, and philosophers, of which he painted many, with qualities of individual humanity. His respect for the dignity of the single human being paved the way for the work of his famous compatriates Diego Velázquez and Francisco Goya. Since his own age, his paintings have been very highly regarded and frequently copied.

Georges Rouault, French, 1871–1958 Early in his career, Rouault was an apprentice to a stained-glass maker, and this training greatly influenced his style. The bitter and sorrowful depictions of clowns, judges, and prostitutes that marked his early years gave way to some of the most profound religious expressions of the 20th century. The suffering of Christ was a recurring theme. *Miserere*, his series of some 60 prints on this subject, made his work available to many collectors who could not have afforded his paintings.

Peter Paul Rubens, Flemish, 1577–1640 The most illustrious artist of his age, Rubens began his career in 1598 in Antwerp, then went to Italy to serve the court of the Gonzaga family in Mantua. On a diplomatic mission for his patrons, he painted in Spain, where he influenced the young Velázquez. From 1608, he resided in Antwerp, where he had an enormous studio with many students and assistants. He was showered with honors during his lifetime and lived like a prince under the patronage of the archdukes who ruled Flanders for the Spanish crown.

Albert Pinkham Ryder, American, 1847–1917 One of America's greatest and most original artists, Ryder developed a Romantic style based on literary themes. The Bible, the operas of Wagner, and the works of Chaucer, Shakespeare, Byron, Tennyson, and Poe particularly attracted him. He was able to portray monumental ideas and the forces of nature on an intimate scale, using simple but strong forms and rich and luminous colors.

Giovanni Girolamo Savoldo, Italian, ca. 1480–after 1548 A relatively unknown master who worked primarily in Venice, Giovanni Girolamo Savoldo did not achieve great success during his lifetime. Today his nocturnal scenes are highly regarded.

Henry Ossawa Tanner, American, 1859–1937 The son of a bishop of the African Methodist Episcopal Church, Tanner painted biblical subjects his entire life but also was known for his landscapes and genre scenes. A student and close friend of Thomas Eakins, arguably the greatest American painter of the 19th century, Tanner had difficulty establishing a career until 1891, when patrons made it possible for him to study further in Europe. After training in Paris and traveling in the Holy Land, Egypt, and Morocco, he settled in Paris and remained there until his death.

Giandomenico Tiepolo, Italian, 1727–1804 The son of Giovanni Battista Tiepolo, Giandomenico assisted his father in his work as the major palace decorator of his day. After Giovanni Battista's death, the younger Tiepolo carried on in his father's tradition, bringing the grand but sweet style of the Venetian Rococo into the first years of the 19th century. Although his work in many instances is almost indistinguishable from that of his father, he displayed a talent and originality in printmaking that was unsurpassed in his era.

Giovanni Battista Tiepolo, Italian, 1696–1770 The elder Tiepolo dominated European art during the 18th century. Among his major works were massive decorative schemes, first for many of the palaces in his native Venice, and later for the King of Sweden, the Prince Archbishop of Würzburg, Germany, and the King of Spain. While he was most adept at frescoes, he also painted numerous portable canvases. No matter how grand his treatment of a subject, his works were always filled with light and imbued with a basically sunny approach to life.

Joseph Mallord William Turner, English, 1775–1851 Turner's unique vision had a significant impact on landscape painting and was a major source of inspiration for the Impressionists. He derived his ideas from those of Claude Lorrain, making the effects of light his primary subject. Like Claude, he referred to historical or topical subjects in his works, but they were secondary to his treatment of luminosity and atmosphere. The brushwork and brilliant vortices of light in his late paintings come close to pure abstraction.

Elihu Vedder, American, 1836–1923 An expatriate American who worked and lived primarily in Rome, Vedder painted highly symbolic and allegorical works. Though he was not highly regarded by his countrymen at the start of his career, he eventually received important commissions for murals in a number of U.S. public buildings, including the Library of Congress. His illustrated 1884 edition of *The Rubáiyát of Omar Khayyám* was one of the most beautiful books produced during the 19th century.

Diego Velázquez, Spanish, 1599–1660 Recent critics have called him the greatest painter in the history of Western art, a reputation only slightly more exalted than the one he enjoyed in his own lifetime. Highly talented at an early age, Velázquez came to the attention of King Philip IV of Spain, who appointed him his sole court portrait painter. The King was younger than the artist and came to depend on him as a warm confidant,

raising him to increasingly more responsible positions in his personal service. He was in charge of the royal collections and was able to travel to Italy to seek art. In addition to portraits of the royal family, Velázquez painted mythological and religious scenes.

Émile-Jean-Horace Vernet, French, 1789–1863 A prolific painter of military subjects, Vernet came from a distinguished family of artists. His most famous works were of Napoleonic battles, but he also painted animal and oriental subjects.

Paolo Veronese, Italian, 1528–1588 One of the greatest Venetian artists of his day (Titian and Tintoretto were his contemporaries), Veronese was the most interested in the human figure, striving to give it volume but not great weight. He executed a large number of lengthy series of religious narratives for various churches and is famous for his banquet scenes. He had many assistants, including his brothers Zelotti and Ponchino.

Jan Victors, Dutch, 1619–1676 Jan Victors was one of the most important artists to study with Rembrandt. He followed his teacher's style for many years, painting mainly religious subjects, but in the 1650s he forged his own approach to the painting of genre subjects.

Jacopo Vignali, Italian, 1592–1664 Little is known of Jacopo Vignali's life, but his works indicate that he was one of the best colorists of the Florentine school.

Benjamin West, American, 1738–1820 West began his career as a portrait painter in Philadelphia and New York. Before he was 22 he had moved to Rome, but eventually he settled in England, where George III became his patron. When he painted scenes of recent history in modern dress for the palace, it was a shocking innovation. He helped found the Royal Academy and, in 1792, succeeded Sir Joshua Reynolds as its president.

Konrad Witz, German, ca. 1400–1444/6 Only a few paintings today are attributed to Konrad Witz. Born in Germany but active primarily in Switzerland, he forged a style that was more naturalistic than the norm for his day and he is credited with the creation of one of the earliest recognizable landscape paintings in art (1444).

Joachim Antoniszoon Wtewael, Dutch, ca. 1566–1638 One of the leading Dutch exponents of Mannerism, Wtewael spent most of his career in Utrecht. His charming, artificial style with its elongated, elegant figures never gave way to the more naturalistic trends in art that emerged during his lifetime.

ALLORI, CRISTOFANO
Judith with the head of Holofernes 163
ALLSTON, WASHINGTON
Elijah in the Dessert 143
ANDREA DEL CASTAGNO
The Youthful David 120
BACCHIACCA
The Gathering of Manna 90
BALDUNG GRIEN, HANS
The Deluge 26-27
BENTON, THOMAS HART
Susanna and the Elders 165
BIAGIO DI ANTONIO
The Story of Joseph 74-75
BONIFAZIO DE' PITATI
Lot and His Daughters 42
BOSCH, HIERONYMUS
The Garden of Paradise 16-17
BRAVO, CECCO
Balaam and the Ass 106
BRAY, JAN DE
David Dances Before the Ark of the Covenant 126
BREENBERGH, BARTHOLOMEUS
Elisha and the Children 146-147
BROWN, FORD MADOX
Elijah Restoring the Widow's Son 144
BRUEGEL THE ELDER, JAN (SEE RUBENS AND BRUEGEL)
BRUEGEL THE ELDER, PIETER
The Suicide of Saul 124-125
BURGKMAIR THE ELDER, HANS
Queen Esther Pleads with Her Husband Ahasuerus for the Rescue of the Jewish People 132-133
CASTELLO, VALERIO
Samson and Delilah 110-111
CHAGALL, MARC
Moses Receiving the Tablets of the Law 96
CONEGLIANO, CIMA DA
David and Jonathan 121
CORINTH, LOVIS
The Arrest and Blinding of Samson 113
CORTONA, PIETRO DA
Hagar and the Angel 46-47
CRANACH THE ELDER, LUCAS
Pharaoh's Hosts Engulfed in the Red Sea 89
DAUGHERTY, JAMES
Job 149
DROST, WILLEM
Ruth and Naomi 64
DÜRER, ALBRECHT
Adam and Eve 18-19
EECKHOUT, GERBRANDT VAN DEN
Elisha and the Shunammite Woman 148
ELSHEIMER, ADAM (FOLLOWER OF)
Tobias and the Angel 168
FERRARI, GAUDENZIO
Abraham and the Three Angels 38-39
FIELD, ERASTUS SALISBURY
The Burial of the Firstborn of Egypt 84
FUSELI, HENRY
The Creation of Eve 12

GAUGUIN, PAUL
Jacob Wrestling with the Angel 60-61
GÉRARD, BARON FRANÇOIS-PASCAL-SIMON
Joseph Recognized by His Brothers 70-71
GIORGIONE
The Trial of Moses by Fire 82
GIOVANNI DI PAOLO
The Creation and Expulsion of Adam and Eve from Paradise 22-23
GUERCINO
Amnon and Tamar 128-129
HENNER, JEAN-JACQUES
The Levite of Ephraim and His Dead Wife 115
HICKS, EDWARD
Peaceable Kingdom 170
HONDECOETER, MELCHIOR DE
Animals from Noah's Ark 32
HUNT, WILLIAM HOLMAN
The Scapegoat 102
JORDAENS, JACOB
Moses Striking Water from the Rock 95
Susanna and the Elders 163, 166-167
KANDINSKY, WASSILY
Improvisation Deluge 30-31
LE BRUN, CHARLES
The Brazen Serpent 103
LIPPI, FILIPPINO
The Worship of the Egyptian Bull-God Apis (Golden Calf) 99-101
LORRAIN, CLAUDE
Landscape with the Marriage of Isaac and Rebecca 54-55
LUCAS VAN LEYDEN
The Worship of the Golden Calf 98
MANTEGNA, ANDREA
Esther and Mordecai 130
MASTER OF THE MANSI MAGDALEN
Judith and the Infant Hercules 162
MASTER OF THE TWELVE APOSTLES
Jacob and Rachel at the Well 58
MEMLING, HANS
Bathsheba at Her Bath 127
MICHELANGELO BUONARROTI
God Dividing the Waters and the Earth 10-11
MIERIS, FRANS VAN, I
Jacob's Dream 57
MILLET, JEAN-FRANÇOIS
Hagar and Ishmael 44-45
Harvesters Resting (Ruth and Boaz) 119
MOEYAERT, CLAES CORNELISZOON
Manoah's Sacrifice 108
MOREAU, GUSTAVE
Delilah 109
MUNCH, EDVARD
Adam and Eve Under the Apple Tree 20-21
MURILLO, BARTOLOMÉ ESTEBAN
Joseph and Potiphar's Wife 66-67
NATOIRE, CHARLES JOSEPH
Adam and Eve After the Fall 24
PELLEGRINI, GIOVANNI ANTONIO
Rebecca at the Well 51
PERUGINO, PIETRO
The Prophet Isaiah 150
PIAZZETTA, GIOVANNI BATTISTA
Elijah Taken Up in a Chariot of Fire 145
PONTORMO, JACOPO DA
Joseph in Egypt 72
POUSSIN, NICOLAS
Manna from Heaven 91-93
The Triumph of David 122-123

The Judgment of Solomon 136-137
POYNTER, SIR EDWARD JOHN
The Visit of the Queen of Sheba to King Solomon 140-141
PUVIS DE CHAVANNES, PIERRE
[Esau's] Return from the Hunt 56
RAPHAEL
The Vision of Ezekiel 151
REMBRANDT VAN RIJN
Jacob's Blessing 76-77
The Blinding of Samson 112
The Prophet Jeremiah Lamenting the Destruction of Jerusalem (Rembrandt's Father) 152
Belshazzar Sees the Writing on the Wall 154-155
RIBERA, JOSÉ DE
Moses 97
ROUAULT, GEORGES
Samson Turning the Millstone 114
RUBENS, PETER PAUL AND BRUEGEL THE ELDER, JAN
Adam and Eve in Paradise 13-15
RUBENS, PETER PAUL
The Meeting of Abraham and Melchizedek 36-37
Lot's Flight from Sodom 40-41
Daniel in the Lions' Den 157
RYDER, ALBERT PINKHAM
Jonah 158-159
SAVOLDO, GIOVANNI GIROLAMO
Elijah Fed by the Raven 142
TANNER, HENRY OSSAWA
Daniel in the Lions' Den 156
TIEPOLO, GIANDOMENICO
The Sacrifice of Isaac 48-49
TIEPOLO, GIOVANNI BATTISTA
Joseph Receiving Pharoah's Ring 68-69
TURNER, JOSEPH MALLORD WILLIAM
The Evening of the Deluge 28
The Fifth Plague of Egypt 85-87
VEDDER, ELIHU
Adam and Eve Mourning the Death of Abel 25
VELAZQUEZ, DIEGO
Jacob Receiving Joseph's Blood-Stained Coat 64-65
VERNET, EMILE-JEAN-HORACE
Abraham Turning Away Hagar 43
VERONESE, PAOLO
Rebecca at the Well 52-53
Jacob and Rachel at the Well 59
The Finding of Moses 80
VICTORS, JAN
Jacob Asks Forgiveness of Esau 62-63
VIGNALI, JACOPO
Moses at the Burning Bush 83
WEST, BENJAMIN
Noah Sacrificing 33
Pharaoh and His Host Lost in the Red Sea 88
WITZ, KONRAD
The Queen of Sheba Before Solomon 138
WTEWAEL, JOACHIM ANTONISZOON
Moses Striking the Rock 94